Phyllis Fender and Randall Bell

Blessings ♥
Phyllis Fender

Leo and Phyllis Fender

Keith Richards and Phyllis Fender, when Keith
presented the award for Leo's induction into the Rock
and Roll Hall of Fame

Randall Bell with a prototype guitar in Leo's lab, and wearing
Leo's famous "peeper" glasses

Phyllis Fender's son Paul, Phyllis, Jaryd Conway and
Randall Bell at the G&L plant

Phyllis Fender with a beautiful picture of Leo
at the Fullerton Museum

Phyllis Fender in Leo's "lab"

PRAISE FOR *LEO FENDER*

When other companies made electric guitars, that is all they did, but Leo had the whole concept in mind: he made an amplifier to match the guitar. It is, after all, electric! This left the other guys with only half an egg. If you also used a Fender amp, you had the whole deal. So simple, so complete, whether you preferred a Stratocaster or a Telecaster. Sturdy, reliable, and beautifully made, Fender remains the standard that others strive to reach—let alone the bass!

— **KEITH RICHARDS, THE ROLLING STONES**

The Leo Fender legacy has continued for decades here at the G&L factory on Fender Avenue in Fullerton, California, where Leo's office and laboratory remind us of his genius and passion for creating tools for musical expression. Though much has been written about his instruments, amplifiers and the musical revolution they fostered, precious little has been shared about this complex man who was brilliant yet humble, competitive yet compassionate, pragmatic yet spiritual. This book is an absolute must read for any music fan, a unique vantage point from which we can more richly understand and appreciate the father of modern music.

— **DAVE MCLAREN, CEO, G&L MUSICAL INSTRUMENTS**

Leo once told Phyllis that all artists are angels and his job was to give them wings to fly. Leo's vision has guided Fender for nearly 70 years. I think about what Leo said every morning on my way to the office and it makes me smile.

— **ANDY MOONEY, CEO, FENDER MUSICAL INSTRUMENTS**

With unwavering support from Randall Bell, Phyllis Fender's book is a love letter to Leo Fender and to a bygone era. Through funny and intimate stories, she takes us to the man behind the Telecaster, the Stratocaster and the myriad of inventions that shaped music in the last half of the 20th century. Other books cover the inventions—this one dwells on their creator.

— **VALERIE MILANO, EDITOR, *THE HOLLYWOOD TIMES***

For every young boy like myself or young girl that was influenced by Rock 'n Roll, and maybe were even fortunate to own a Fender Guitar, the story and history of Leo Fender becomes personal. Leo's wife, Phyllis and Dr. Randall Bell reveal his subtle, humble and productive renown. Leo's gift and passion are the perfect story and example of when need meets invention. Rock 'n Roll was born and it needed a parent that would give it a signature sound and instrument. Iconic Fender guitars were born for Rock 'n Roll as much as Rock 'n Roll was born for Fender. As Phyllis Fender says, this is a love story of Leo and his kids and will cause you to fall in love with your Fender guitar again.

— **BILL MARTINEZ, RADIO HOST, *BILL MARTINEZ LIVE***

As a longtime guitar player and the owner of many vintage Fender instruments and amplifiers, I was delighted to learn more about the man behind the legendary company. One of the "friendliest" signatures in the world, comes to life in this amazing behind-the-scenes glimpse into the life of Leo Fender.

— **ROB SCHILLING, HOST OF WINA'S *THE SCHILLING SHOW***

The embodiment of the American exceptionalism that won the Cold War and defined the 20th century, Leo Fender's life is essential knowledge for anyone who wishes to understand freedom in the United States, and in the world.

— **JOHN LAFAYETTE RAMEY, MUSICIAN, JOURNALIST**

Many books have been written about Leo Fender and his marvelous musical inventions, but none have given us a glimpse into Fender's personal life. Phyllis Fender and Randall Bell have done an incredible job of humanizing the genius that was Leo Fender as his legacy continues!

— ERIC DAHL, FOX 17 *ROCK & REVIEW*

A must read for any person who has ever plugged into an amplifier or dreamed of becoming an entrepreneur. We get a unique view under the hood of the selfless utilitarian genius who worked tirelessly around the clock up until his final days to perfect the craft. Phyllis Fender takes us behind the scenes of the man who worked famously behind the scenes for one reason alone—to serve the musician. A true underdog story.

— MATT GIBNEY, *THE STRATOSPHERE*

This short yet captivating book is required reading for any true Fender afficionado. While much has been written about the work of Clarence Leonidas "Leo" Fender, precious little has been written about Leo Fender the man. This book is a game changer.

— VAUGHN SKOW, *VINTAGE GUITAR MAGAZINE*

You've heard of the Wizard of Waukesha? How about Leo the Lion from Fullerton? In the movie 'It's A Wonderful Life', George Bailey was shown by Clarence the Angel what things would have looked like had George never been born. I would hate to see what the world would look like without Leo Fender. A one-eyed radio repairman—born in a barn—transformed the world with one guitar. This is his story captured in an uncommon and absorbing way.

— BRYAN LOCKE, BOWLING GREEN'S CLASSIC ROCK D93
DAILY NEWS BROADCASTING CO., INC.

Phyllis Fender provides a beautifully candid portrait of the humble genius we all know as the inventor of the electric guitar in *Leo Fender: The Quiet Giant Heard Around the World*. From losing an eye in a childhood accident, to achieving fame and fortune through his infamous inventions, Fender's life had plenty of ups and downs. But the one thing that remained the same through all of it was Leo; unfaltering, stoic, and supremely dedicated to his craft.

— TREVOR ENGLISH, WAREHOUSE GUITAR SPEAKERS

Phyllis Fender lovingly refers to Leo Fender throughout the book as "my Leo." The book is not all about the guitars. It's about Leo Fender the man. It's easy to read, full of history, and features black and white photos throughout. Reading this book, being involved in the music industry, and having lived in Southern California, I thoroughly enjoyed the photos and history of Fullerton. I recommend the book for anyone wanting to learn more about the man behind this iconic brand.

— TARA LOW, *GUITAR GIRL MAGAZINE*

As devotees of both music and technology, it was such a treat to dive into the world of Leo Fender with both Phyllis and Randall. Leo was a visionary who has changed the world of music—and technology—as we know it today. This book took us back in time, and really told stories in such a way that we felt that we were there. Thank you, Phyllis and Randall. We're forever grateful for your storytelling and warm hearts!

— GEEKS & BEATS

Any guitar player who appreciates Fender guitars and amps will appreciate learning more about the unusual man behind them, Leo Fender. This book, by Leo's second wife, offers an admittedly biased view of Leo the single-minded inventor. While short on details about specific instruments and amps, it's long on personal anecdotes and details of his life as only a loving wife can offer.

— CHRIS BEYTES, BALL PUBLISHING
(AND PROUD OWNER OF A '57 STRAT REISSUE)

Leo Fender

THE QUIET GIANT HEARD AROUND THE WORLD

Leo Fender: The Quiet Giant Heard Around the World

Phyllis Fender & Randall Bell, PhD

Distributed by Ingram Publisher Services, LLC - Berkeley, California, USA

ISBN: 978-0-996793-14-8

Library of Congress Control Number: 2017938663

Printed in the United States of America

10 9 8 7 6 5 4 3 2 1

Photo Credits:

Rufus Chaka © Bobby Holland / mptvimages.com
Louis Johnson and Leo Fender © Bobby Holland / mptvimages.com
Elvis mptvimages.com
Buddy Holly mptvimages.com
Jimmy Page © Richard E. Aaron / mptvimages.com
Jackson 5 © Michael Jones / mptvimages.com
Jimmy Hendrix Photo by D A Pennebaker. Photo courtesy of Pennebaker Hegedus Films, The Monterey International Pop Foundation Inc. and Arthouse18
Keith Richards © Jane Rose

To contact the publisher or authors, please visit *LeoFender.com*

CONTENTS

A Note from Phyllis Fender

There are so many who have helped and supported both Leo and me over the years.

Richard Smith was a friend of Leo's and mine and was the curator of the Fullerton Museum Center for some time. Leo liked Richard because he was not a yes-man and spoke up to tell it the way it was. Richard is a true historian of all things Fender, and his input and help has always been appreciated. Randy Bell and I first met at the Fullerton Museum at an event organized by Kelly Chidester. Kelly has always been so supportive.

I also want to thank all the great people at G&L on Fender Avenue in Fullerton. They have kept much of Leo's office as he left it on the day he passed away, and they always go out of their way to preserve Leo's legacy of producing quality guitars. They have graciously provided access to the manufacturing facilities and Leo's office. Stepping in there makes me feel like I am stepping back into Leo's world, and that was so helpful as I began writing this book.

Everyone from the CEO to the janitor at Fender Musical Instruments have been wonderful, and very kind. I appreciate that they and G&L keep spreading the joy of Leo's wonderful guitars around the world. The guitars on the cover of this book have great historical significance. I would also like to thank Gilbert Ramirez for carting the guitars around and for taking such great care of them, as we created the cover or used them for inspiration as we met.

Within this book, I will share some biographical information, experiences with Leo's friends and employees, along with many stories from our life together, all in the hopes that you get to meet the Leo I loved.

This book was written over months, while Randy and I regularly met in our private office, which was a booth at the back wall of Polly's Pies, on Raymond Avenue in Fullerton. Polly's cooks prepared the delicious food and pies that fueled the writing of this book, and the servers have just been wonderful! One day, a twelve-year-old boy Luke walked up to our table and introduced himself. In the third grade he had written a report on Leo, when he discovered that his home had once belonged to Leo in his early years. His discovery helped to fill a gap of Leo's history. What a little angel that boy was!

I would like to thank both my family and the Bell family for allowing us the many hours to write this book and bring this side of Leo to the world. Our families even took a whole day to tour all of Leo's sites listed in the Appendix, including Randy's ninety-five-year-old mother, Frances. She was such a trooper! I want to thank the small army of readers who were kind enough to read the initial manuscripts and offer suggestions. This includes Susan Kaneshiro, Lynette Bartlomain, Frances Bell, Alex Wohl, Chris Sheffield, Anita Lowe, Jim Bell, Bobbie Caraway, Barbara Dyvig, and many other friends and family members too numerous to mention.

Lastly, to Leo himself, who gave me many years of wonderful memories which enabled me to write his story with Randy. Love and hugs, Leo!

A Note from Randall Bell

It was a privilege to work on this book with Mrs. Fender.

Like so many, I still remember the thrill of unwrapping my first Fender guitar at Christmas. Not only did I love the guitars, but Fender was interwoven into my daily life as a kid. My father led the research and development there. He was a mechanical engineer, complete with a plastic pocket protector, and he loved every minute he worked there. Dad made our kitchen table out of cutaway Stratocaster wood, which we also piled high in the garage and used for bonfires at the beach.

The Fender plant was right down the street, and I went there all the time. Dad introduced me to every person on the production line, where they explained their individual craft in detail. It was an extended family, and Freddie Tavares and his wife Tamar, even played at my sister's wedding.

Later, my father made my daughter Britten's dollhouse out of scrap rosewood used for fretboards. I joke that it is the only Fender dollhouse in the world! My parents both had the highest regard for everyone at the company and admired the Fenders themselves, who lived in our neighborhood.

I get it with Leo. My dad and Leo were cut out of the same cloth. Few know who my father is because he was much like Leo. He never showed off. At Fender, everyone was like that. Dad would spend all day with the world's biggest rock stars and not mention a word about it unless my brother or I hounded him. I begged him to let me know when Jimmy Page would come in, but he didn't budge.

The world's icons teach us so much; however, we hit the jackpot with Mr. and Mrs. Fender. Leo is a goldmine of inspiration, and was a class act on every level. I wish that everyone could have the pleasure of meeting Mrs. Fender. Leo was so quiet, that as a kid I likely walked by him many times and never knew it. Yet, Mrs. Fender has never met a microphone that she didn't like, and that's great news for all of us! She has a spectacular sense of humor, a gift for storytelling, and a heart of gold. Honestly, I have listened to her for two or three hours at a time—and it is pure joy. Sometimes we laughed and sometimes we cried. Other times, we laughed so hard we cried!

We had so much fun writing this book. We sat for hours in our "office" at Polly's Pies, went over documents, studied the items in Leo's office, sorted through photo albums, and stood together to watch the craftsmen at G&L paint my guitar, certainly the most beautiful I have ever seen. We ran all over Fullerton together, exploring the Leo sites. It has been pure bliss.

Mr. and Mrs. Fender are music royalty. She did so much for Leo, and we all are fortunate to have her tell us the inside story. Her family—Paul, Chris, and Jon—have been supportive of their mother and this project. I have immeasurable respect for Mr. and Mrs. Fender. I hope that everyone gets the same joy I have from learning about these two remarkable lives.

CHAPTER 1

The Real Deal

O ccasionally, the world produces one of those rare thinkers that alters the course of history. Disney reinvented entertainment, Einstein revolutionized science, Edison lit up our lives with the light bulb, Guttenberg spread knowledge with the printing press, Bell got the world talking with the telephone—and Fender revolutionized music.

If you think about it for a moment, Leo Fender has influenced every person on earth today—at least everyone who has ever heard a song.

Guitar Player magazine declared that Clarence "Leo" Fender is the father of the solid body guitar. Leo's guitars have been used by everyone from Elvis Presley to Eric Clapton and from Jimmy Page to Jimmy Hendrix. *Rolling Stone* magazine published a list of the world's top 100 guitarists, and 91 of them used one of Leo's guitars on stage. The others used guitars that copied Leo's inventions and concepts.

The highest price ever spent on music memorabilia was not for Michael Jackson's glove, original Beatles' handwritten lyrics or even one of Elvis' killer pantsuits. It was for a Fender Stratocaster, which sold for a staggering $2.7 million in 2005.

Buddy Holly played a Fender; in fact, there is a picture of his favorite Fender guitar on his gravestone. It's ironic—they spelled Buddy's name wrong, but they got the guitar right!

We know so much about so many great lives, but so little about Leo Fender. While the Fender name is known around the world, as an iconic brand practically worshiped by musicians, Leo himself largely remains an enigma. Inside of this little curmudgeon running around the world, there was another side of Leo that most people never saw.

As his wife, that is the side I want to share with everyone. I love guitars. To me, they are beautiful works of art. However, there are already lots of wonderful books written about Leo's guitars. This book is less about guitars, but more about the man who invented them. This is the story that has never really been told, as my Leo was famously quiet. Leo was certainly not one to toot his own horn and rarely talked to reporters.

Elvis and his Stratocaster with Ann Margaret in "Viva Las Vegas"

Leo was never rude, but he rarely gave autographs or posed for pictures. He was not big on chit chat. He simply had other things on his mind, so very few people really got to know him. Leo turned down hundreds of requests for media interviews, yet thankfully he opened up for *Guitar Player* magazine in 1978. It is interesting that he turned down national, mainstream television, magazines, and radio. He had no interest in interviews on the Tonight Show, the Wall Street Journal, or 60 Minutes, but he did take the time to talk directly to guitar players through a trade magazine. Leo loved guitar players!

A parade of rock stars and country music legends often visited the Fender and G&L plants. While they all wanted to meet Leo, he was usually too busy designing his next guitar. On one such occasion, Prince refused to leave the G&L plant without meeting Leo, so the team nervously went back to Leo's office and pleaded with him to come out and speak to him. Leo reluctantly agreed. Prince asked Leo to promise never to make another purple guitar like his. Leo simply smiled and said, "Sure, I'll do that," and turned around and walked right back into his office.

Leo was different. He was 100% authentic and a purist for his passion for musical instruments. He only shared his deeper emotions at home. He shunned the typical trappings of wealth and fame. His dedication to his personal mission to make his next guitar even better was so pure, that every daily activity centered on getting into his beloved laboratory to design the world's greatest instruments.

Leo never created a guitar, amp, or other musical instrument for himself. He could not play a guitar, or even tune a guitar. For health reasons, he reluctantly sold his first company, for a fortune. Yet with millions in the bank, he continued living in a mobile home so that he could run his life with a minimum of distraction. Leo was the real deal, and he stayed true to his love for his instruments and to those who played them. If I had to pick one word to describe Leo, it would be *authentic*.

Leo Fender did not do any of this for his own glory. Leo loved music, and he crafted musical instruments for you and me so that we could all enjoy the power of great music. Leo truly thought of musicians as the angels who made the world a better place, and he simply wanted to support them. Whenever he spoke to musicians, he always carefully listened and incorporated their feedback into his next invention.

Think about all the great memories in life. The high school prom, driving down the highway with the windows down and listening to your favorite song, a beautiful wedding, a fun party, a smooth jazz club, or an insane rock concert. Leo's influence was there. Leo is everywhere. Now, for the first time ever, we will enter the real world of Mr. Leo Fender.

To truly understand Leo, you must know that he challenged conventional thinking. Leo felt that conventional wisdom would get conventional results, and he demanded something much bigger. He knew exactly what he wanted and how to get there. One thing Leo knew for sure was that he was not following anyone else's path in life. He would blaze his own trail. Very few people accomplish something iconic and change the world the way my Leo did.

This man had a deep confidence in who he was and was nothing short of a man on a mission. This story needs to be told because those who think they know about Leo typically only have heard that he was a certified workaholic. That was true, but he was more than that. He was also a man with a keen sense of purpose, and his intensity for work was so extreme it became comical. Sometimes, Leo's work ethic even bordered on insanity. Like many of history's great figures, Leo did not do his thing by falling into line. He had his own distinct style, and he always stayed true to it.

At home, he had a lighter side and a keen sense of humor. We laughed and laughed together. He absolutely loved to do things with our family. Even more than guitars, he was enthralled by our grandchildren, and he would cry when the time came for them to go home. Near the end of his life, he reconciled his Christian beliefs.

Leo walked to his own beat and had a hard time taking orders from anyone. In business, he was an executive with a screwdriver.

Leo never wanted to impress anybody. He wanted people to enjoy his instruments. That was the source of his pride. Work was his real joy.

Keith Richards

Leo was a wonderful husband, and we were best friends. We loved to go on cruises, and we shared many adventures together. Our life was so different than everybody else's. Opposites attract. Here is this quiet genius always thinking, and then there's me, who just cannot stop talking. I am very outgoing, and I have many friends. I love to see people, and I am excited when they call me on the phone. If I told Leo, "We are going to have a party!" Leo would say, pretending to be annoyed, "Oh, no, not again!" The whole thing did not make sense to most people, but it made sense to us.

Over twenty years ago, because of a heart condition, a doctor told me that my heart was pumping at 17% of normal and that I only had three to six months to live. I wanted a second opinion, but the other doctor said the same thing. I did not believe either one of them, and today those two doctors are dead! My heart just keeps ticking because I need to finally tell the story of this man that I love so much!

Leo was not much of a talker, but I am! So here we go!

CHAPTER 2

The Early Years

Leo was not the type of man who dwelled on the past. Nor did he speak about his childhood, unless he was provoked. So, that is exactly what I did!

Over the years, I coaxed Leo countless times to tell me his stories, either over dinner or while on a cruise, and usually after some persistence he did talk. It was fun seeing him just being Leo, thinking and being quiet. I would ask him a question and watch as he reluctantly thought back. I prodded him for more, and then I would watch his face finally light up with a wonderful story. His stories would make us either laugh or cry, but mostly laugh! So, let's start at the beginning.

Leo Fender was born in a barn, literally.

On the corner of Harbor Boulevard and La Palma Avenue, in an unincorporated area of Orange County that was then called Fullerton, stood the Lone Oak Farm. It was named the Lone Oak Farm because it was largely dirt and vegetable patches, except for one huge oak tree that stood near the center.

It was a simple farm, with long rows of carrots, celery, lettuce, potatoes, tomatoes, and lots of other vegetables and fruits. There were many other farms nearby, mainly orange groves and strawberry patches. A flatbed truck was parked near the farm's only structure, a wooden barn which housed the tools and workbenches. It also housed a family—until they got around to buying more lumber and building a house.

The original Fender Radio Shop on Harbor Boulevard

Inside that barn, on August 10, 1909, Clarence Monte Fender and Harriet Elvira Wood became parents of a little boy, whom they named Clarence Leonidas Fender, or "Leo." This couple needed Leo because there was a lot of work to do on the farm.

Little did Mr. and Mrs. Fender know that one day this boy would go on to win a Grammy Award, Academy of Country Music Awards, and a Cliffie Stone Pioneer Award. He would be the Grand Marshal at parades and would be inducted into the Rock and Roll Hall of Fame. They had never heard of rock and roll. Nobody had—because it had not been invented yet. The world needed Leo to pave the way.

As the family grew with the addition of a sister, Wilda, the place became known as the Fender Farm. It fronted a street that would one day be named Harbor Boulevard. Just across the street, a guy named Karl Karcher would one day start his very first hamburger joint, and call it Carl's Jr.

Just a short drive south on Harbor Boulevard, another guy would start the world's first theme park. His name was Walt Disney. To top it off, just a few blocks to the north, in a little radio repair shop located at 107 N. Harbor Boulevard, Leo Fender would one day invent the world's first modern electric guitar.

You will never find a street like Harbor Boulevard anywhere else in the world. If you want to do something great, I suggest you do it on Harbor Boulevard. There is something magical about that street!

Leo in front of his business

Harbor Boulevard was the place where Leo grew up and was taught a strong, strict work ethic. He was given chores to do from the moment he could walk. When he turned five, he was sent off to Orangethorpe Elementary School a few blocks to the north. He loved going to school because, the moment he got home, there were more chores. He had to hoe the ground into long furrows, plant the seeds, water the crops, pick and clean the vegetables, and carefully pack and load them onto the family's flatbed truck.

Leo had a very strict father and mother. The German traits of the family taught him to be thrifty and hard working. Leo was taught that you really should not take too much pleasure in life. You should always be working.

It was a different age. There was no time for Little League baseball, skate boards, or lollygagging around. Leo only went to church a few times, and, when he heard that the treasurer had taken off with the congregation's money, Leo announced that, if this is how Christians behaved, he did not want anything to do with it. Church was not for him. Leo turned his focus to his work.

Leo kept the fences in repair and did any other chore that came along. He winced when his Father often told him, "Leo, you are only as good as the work that you do!" Leo grew up in a family that was too busy to fuss over birthdays. Christmas was a meager affair. Imagine never having a birthday party. This was not the kind of love that every boy needed, but Leo had a home, and plenty of good, fresh farm food to eat.

When Leo was about seven or eight, tragedy struck. It was dark, and Leo was washing down the family's truck. It had been used to take a load of vegetables to the market, and was filthy from squashed tomatoes and stray leaves of lettuce. As he was scrubbing away, Leo's foot slipped off the edge of the flatbed and he fell off the truck. In the darkness, he did not see the picket fence, which got him right in the right eye. Leo lost the eye, which was later replaced with a matching, beautiful blue glass eye.

Leo did not complain, and he was not bitter about losing his eye. In fact, I never heard Leo get angry, cuss or yell. He was never moody or temperamental. That was not his style. Leo was just a solid, mild, steady, honest guy. He just worked hard on his chores, his schoolwork, and did his part to help support his family and their farm.

Jimi Hendrix

When the truck was clean, and the chores were done, Leo's dad would allow him to go into the barn and do his favorite thing, which was to dissect anything mechanical. Leo simply loved figuring out anything that could be taken apart with a screwdriver. At an early age, Leo learned the great benefits of having a screwdriver in his shirt pocket, a habit he kept his entire life. I think that plastic pocket protectors were first made for Leo. For him, they were always in style.

When Leo was about thirteen years old, his uncle ran a repair shop up the California coast in Santa Maria. His uncle sent him a cardboard box filled up with old radios, alarm clocks, and batteries. Later, Leo went on a family trip to visit his uncle's shop. He was fascinated by a tube radio his uncle had made. Radios were rare, and Leo said that the music he heard on that tube radio made a huge impression on him. Leo immediately started to tinker with, build, and repair radios on the barn's workbench. Soon his workbench interests spread to anything electronic or mechanical, such as alarm clocks, vacuum cleaners, and record players.

While living on the farm, Leo was drawn to music. Leo told me that when he worked in the vegetable fields, he would turn the radio volume way up and listen to Jimmie Rodgers. He learned to play the piano, saxophone, and trumpet. But Leo never pursued a career as a performer. "I wasn't really adapted to it," he said. Generally, Leo liked being at home; he did not want a life on the road.

Leo always took school seriously. He took almost everything seriously. After all, with a glass eye, he had no chance in sports.

The Jackson Five

Besides, Leo was a thinker. In addition to the farm work, Leo did janitorial work in high school. I think that between farm work and janitorial work, he was motived to do well in school and move on.

In September 1928, Leo graduated from Fullerton Union High School on Chapman Avenue in Fullerton. He did not go far for college. In fact, he just crossed the street and enrolled at Fullerton Junior College as an accounting major. Today, the same campus is simply called Fullerton College. While studying accounting, Leo continued to spend his spare time tinkering with radios and anything electric. Remarkably, the creator of the world's first electric guitar never enrolled in an electronics class!

Leo was fascinated with designing, inventing, and building. Next to the old Fullerton College campus, construction started on Plumber Auditorium, which is a beautiful building that still stands to this day. The project immediately caught Leo's attention, and he would sit and do his homework on the lawn while watching the construction. The young man's presence became so predictable that the workers noticed Leo and invited him to come onto the site and watch the construction up close. Leo was a mild-mannered, friendly kid and the workers liked him. He studied every phase of construction, from breaking ground and grading the site to laying the foundation and framing. He intently studied the installation of the electrical system and the roofing. Leo was like a sponge soaking in knowledge, and he asked lots of questions. It became a daily part of his practical learning that supplemented his formal college studies.

After two years, Leo graduated from Fullerton Junior College with an associate's degree in accounting. In those days, very few went to college, so that was a big deal. Leo got a job as a delivery man for Consolidated Ice and Cold Storage Company in Anaheim, but that was not his thing. However, the company saw Leo's real strengths, and he was hired as their bookkeeper.

During this same time, the word was spreading in Fullerton that Leo was good with electronics. A local band asked Leo if he would make a public-address system to use at dances up in Hollywood, and he agreed. Leo ended up building six of these PA systems, which was his very first business venture.

With a college degree and the beginnings of an entrepreneurial flare, Leo was a good catch, and one lady took notice. In 1933, Leo met Esther Klotzly, and they were married in 1934. Leo got another job working as an accountant for the California Highway Department up the coast in San Luis Obispo. During the Depression, Leo was laid off, but he was hired again, this time as an accountant for a tire company. After only about six months, all the accountants, including Leo, were laid off. By this time, Leo realized that accounting was not for him, he wanted to do something else.

Buddy Holly

Despite the Depression and the repeated layoffs, Leo still had drive. In fact, he had lots of drive. The farm upbringing taught him a strong work ethic, selling vegetables at the market taught him some people skills, making tools in the barn taught him woodworking and metalwork, and the accounting work taught him the dollars and cents of business. Studying the daily construction of Plumber Auditorium showed him how to build a facility, his tinkering with radios schooled him in electronics, dissecting alarm clocks showed him the world of mechanical engineering, and building and successfully selling PA systems gave Leo a spark of the entrepreneurial life. Leo knew how to create value and cut costs. He was a practical, hands-on guy. Leo's motto was always, "I'll buy it used, or I'll make it myself."

Jimmy Page

Conventional wisdom says to specialize in one thing. Yet no job was beneath Leo, and no job was too big. Leo did not know it at the time, but his unconventional spectrum of skills provided him with exactly the skills he needed to do something epic!

In 1938, with a young wife to take care of and tired of being laid off, Leo got bold. He borrowed $600 and returned to Fullerton, the hometown he loved. Leo started his own radio repair shop, Fender Radio Service, at 107 S. Harbor Boulevard. Despite a tough childhood just a few blocks to the south, Leo did not want to get away from the town. In fact, he stayed right by the old Fender Farm site. It was part of who he was, and he was okay with it.

Leo worked hard in his new shop, building and repairing radios and record players and doing anything else that leaned toward his interests in music. Soon, musicians heard about Leo and asked him to build more public-address systems. He built, repaired, rented, and sold them. Guitarists also came into Leo's shop to get amplification for their lap guitars and Hawaiian steel guitars, which were coming onto the Southern California music scene.

Leo was happy. He had established a small shop in the town he loved. Music was now a part of his daily work routine. Business was good and getting better. Word was spreading that Leo was the guy for all things electric.

Leo and Esther's first home, just a few blocks from his first shop in Fullerton

CHAPTER 3

The Magic Moment

The moment when Leo Fender got the idea about the electric guitar says a lot about what made him tick.

Germany invaded Poland in 1939, just a year after Leo got married. When the Japanese bombed Pearl Harbor in 1941, millions of men jumped at the chance to serve their country, but Leo was left at home. The Army did not want him because he had a glass eye. This did not sit well with Leo, who knew he could contribute and was always eager to help.

Leo never once complained about his situation, he just quietly kept moving forward. He loved his country, and he wanted to do his part to serve. This meant that he needed to invent a way to do it. That was okay because Leo was an inventor at heart.

In the 1940s, it was common to have war bond dances where the town would come out, sing, dance and hopefully buy some war bonds and stamps to support the troops. One warm summer night, at a park in Fullerton near his high school, Leo figured out how he could help. He was the guy who would set up the dances. He was good with electronics, so he would lay the cables to bring in the electricity, string the lights from tree to tree, set up the microphones and amplifiers for the singers, set up chairs, and quietly get the whole event set up.

Leo typically worked alone, a nondescript, quiet man who was attentive and pleasant and made the place come alive. Content with being in the background, Leo silently enjoyed the setting he created.

When the sun went down, and scores of people flowed into the dance, Leo remained on the sidelines. Leo was always calm, and keenly observant. He stood by in case anything broke or needed his attention. Not being much of a dancer himself, he just enjoyed the simple things, like seeing everyone enjoying themselves, watching the sales of bonds and stamps, and knowing that he was doing his part to support his country.

One warm, Fullerton summer night, everything was going smoothly, so Leo just sat near the band enjoying the music. At the war bond dance, they were mostly playing big band music, and Leo always admired musical talent. While Leo had played the piano and saxophone in high school and college, he no longer played any instruments. Leo knew music took both a special gift and a lot of time. He never really got good himself, but he appreciated those who did. He watched the brass section, tapped his foot to the beat of the drums, and soaked in the beautiful singing.

Then something caught Leo's eye. Leo noticed the guitar players. That was the moment that changed the world forever.

While the guitarists played their wooden, acoustic guitars with all their might, nobody could hear them. They were playing their hearts out, but they were basically invisible! Leo felt bad for them. The guitarists had to be heard! Leo got an idea. He was determined to help these talented musicians be heard, just like the rest of the band.

The whole idea of the electric guitar was sparked by Leo Fender's deep, never-ending desire to help other people. The birth of the electric guitar is a profound story, and it reveals so much about Leo. It was never about Leo, and it would never be about Leo. He simply wanted the underdog to be heard. Little did he know that he was changing the world. He had no idea of the millions of dollars or the international fame that would be coming his way. For Leo, it was all about his deep, authentic passion for helping people.

From setting up for the dance to helping fund a cause he felt so deeply about, to working behind the scenes to make sure everyone had a good time, to the moment he wanted to help a struggling guitarist to get heard, it was never about Leo. In his mind, it was all about helping his country, the dancers, and ultimately the musicians.

Leo in high school

That's the secret to understanding Leo Fender. He knew that helping others made him happy, and he never strayed from that guiding principle.

THE TELECASTER DAYS

The idea to help the struggling guitarists remained Leo's obsession for the rest of his life.

The day after the dance, in 1943, Leo Fender went to his radio shop. He got out some drafting paper and started working on designing a ground-up, solid-body electrical guitar with electrical pickups. Nobody had ever done it before, but that did not stop him. He told me that at his radio shop, he got a hunk of wood, cut the middle, out and put some electronics in it. That is where the magic began. He built several "paddle guitars" that quickly evolved into the guitars we see today.

Leo's high school yearbook

When Leo came out with the electric guitar, he said that people laughed and made fun of him. Scoffing, people called them "boat paddles." Most people do not like being laughed at. Leo did not like it either, but he did not take it personally. He converted that energy into fuel that propelled him forward. Leo believed in himself and in his invention.

Ironically, when Leo's electric guitar took off, the critics went from laughing to trying to take credit. Some manufactured a debate over who really invented the electric guitar, so let's clear that up. At the time that Leo invented the electric guitar, a few people were starting to put pickups on regular acoustic guitars. Leo never claimed to have invented that concept, and some people, including himself, were putting pickups on different things like steel lap guitars. However, Leo got the idea from the war bond dance to put pickups on a solid body piece of wood, and create what today is considered a true electric guitar. When these kinds of discussions came up, Leo would just smile, and calmly say, "I've got the patent."

Leo really had something, but it did not take off immediately. In his rented shop on Harbor Boulevard, Leo bought some parts from Mr. Ellingson, who owned the shop he rented. Leo built guitar after guitar, but they did not sell overnight. After thirty days Mr. Ellingson came to collect on his invoice, and Leo just said, "You can't collect on that bill, I haven't sold the guitar yet." Mr. Ellingson just smiled and tried to explain things to Leo, who as an accountant knew better. However, Leo soon did sell the guitar, and then another and another. And they just kept on selling. Sales may have started off slow, but they quickly picked up. Leo paid his bills.

Leo's first shop is listed on the National Historical Register. It is a good thing too because that building was made from beautiful brick, while all the rest of Leo's buildings were so ugly! Leo just wanted places to get the job done, and he was no interior decorator. The key word for Leo was *function!* From the time Leo started building his own factories, the rest of his buildings were non-descript, grey, concrete block buildings. But I will say that inside those ugly buildings, beautiful things did happen.

Today, at the rear of his first building there is a ceramic mural of a striking red Stratocaster guitar, created by wonderful school children from Fullerton.

While the war was raging, Leo met Clayton Orr "Doc" Kauffman. Doc had been a designer of lap steel guitars in the 1930s for Rickenbacker. Leo talked Doc into teaming up, and they formed the K&F Manufacturing Corporation. In 1944, Leo and Doc patented a lap steel guitar that used a pickup that Leo had patented. Leo would later buy out Doc's interests and rename the company after himself.

Guitar Player magazine said,

> *Clayton Orr "Doc" Kauffman was a key person in Leo's introduction to manufacturing. "Leo came by one day," recalled Doc, "and he said, 'Hey, you've been building guitars around here – want to build some together?' and I said, 'Well, sure, sounds okay to me." Kauffman and Fender called their company K&F and built lap steels and small amps. Doc was dubious about a future in guitar building, despite the modest but promising successes of K&F. "See, it hadn't been that long since the Depression," he explained. "My dad was a credit boy all his life – owed money on the farm – so I told myself that I'd never go into debt. Leo was different – He'd go into debt on an investment like a house afire! He didn't care. Besides, he was smart. And he thinks at it all the time; he keeps digging. He's a pursuer, by day and night. That's what put the guitar where it is.*

I only met Doc a few times, but Leo told me that when Doc had worked for Rickenbacker in Santa Ana, they built Hawaiian and steel lap guitars. Doc had invented a pickup and a tailpiece that Leo called a *tremolo*. Nobody knows where Leo got this name, but he always insisted that everyone call it that. It was not a vibrato, not a whammy bar, but a *tremolo!*

In 1946, Leo set up his first plant to produce his guitars a couple of blocks away from the radio repair shop at 122 S. Pomona Avenue. Today, the site has a parking structure, and over two entrances there are wonderful murals of Leo and his inventions. It was created by a local artist, with the help of some of Fullerton's children.

In 1949, Leo finished a prototype of a thin solid-body electric guitar and commercially released it in 1950 as the Fender Esquire. He renamed it the Broadcaster, but that got Leo into copyright trouble with Gretsch Drums. Leo was not a fighter and not about to waste time with a bunch of lawyers. He just quickly sidestepped and trimmed the name off the decals. Today, those guitars are known as "Nocasters." Eventually, Leo thought of a new name, the Telecaster. This name was a simple, catchy blend between the new, upcoming televisions and radio broadcasters. That was Leo—he liked it simple.

The Telecaster immediately caught on. Leo, now more business savvy from his prior legal challenges, quickly took his drawings and registered them with the US Patent Office. This turned out to be yet another brilliant idea, which kept the copycats at bay. Leo just loved the Telecaster and the music it made. With his one good eye, Leo knew style when he saw it. The Telecaster had style.

When Leo invented the Telecaster, he had his own musical taste in mind. Leo was always clear that he specifically liked three kinds of music. There was country music. There was western music. And there was country-western music. For his entire life, he simply loved watching a Telecaster being played by country-western players.

When I think about the Telecaster, I wonder how many other products were invented in the 1940s that are still considered iconic today? Now, that is "staying power!" That Telecaster later created music ranging from Chuck Berry to the Beatles to Jimmy Page's Led Zeppelin *One* album, and everything in between. Leo's years of obsession with the Telecaster resulted in an instrument that today continues to inspire musicians.

THE STRATOCASTER DAYS

Leo continued working on Pomona Avenue for a few years, but his Telecaster guitar was taking off, and it was clear that he needed more space. Leo insisted that the company stay in Fullerton, so he went a few blocks east and found a large tract of level land on Raymond Avenue.

Leo designed the buildings himself—but then again, he designed everything himself! Leo was optimistic about his business, but he was also cautious. He designed the building as multiple, small independent units that could also be operated as one large manufacturing plant. Leo thought that if his new business ever struggled or failed, at least it would be easy to lease out the individual units. That never happened.

One day, the contractors handed Leo a set of keys to 500 S. Raymond Avenue. It was a non-descript, grey concrete building located just south of the railroad line in the industrial section of Fullerton.

Leo unlocked the doors, turned on the lights and got to work. With a growing business, Leo was on the lookout for talented people. By chance, Leo met Freddie Tavares. He was born on Maui, Hawaii, and was about four years younger than Leo.

It is gutsy of him, but when the two met, Freddie told Leo that his amplifiers were junk. A proud man would have gotten mad and written the guy off, but remember, Leo was not conventional. Many CEOs surround themselves with yes-men who always vote unanimously for everything the leader proposes. Leo was different, and he always liked people that told him the truth.

Leo quietly asked Freddie what was wrong with his amplifiers, and Freddie immediately turned the amp around and started showing Leo various design issues. Leo was impressed with Freddie's insights, and he hired Freddie on the spot. Leo connected with authentic people— people who told it how it really is, had a feel for the business and got the job done.

Freddie had the vibe Leo liked. In fact, Freddie was a Hawaiian version of Leo. Quiet, mellow, and calm, Freddie was also intensely in love with music and musical instruments. While Freddie looked Hawaiian, he was a mix of Portuguese, Hawaiian, Chinese, English, Tahitian, and Samoan. Freddie would sometimes say, "The Portuguese makes me stubborn; Chinese makes me smart; English makes me high-class; Hawaiian gives me the music; Tahitian gives me the beat—I couldn't ask for more!"

On his first day on the job in 1953, Freddie took out some paper and drew a design for Leo. Leo loved it, and together the two of them collaborated to invent the Stratocaster. Freddie not only worked for Leo in the Pre-CBS days, but stayed with the Fender company even during the CBS period as a designer and engineer within the research and development department. While his contributions were huge, Freddie was always very mild and humble. He once said, "All of the guitars were essentially Leo's design."

Leo and I were both quite fond of Freddie and his wife, Tamar. Freddie was the one who played the instruments, and had a knack for truly feeling the instrument as he and his wife sang together. If Freddie liked it, Leo knew it was a winner, and that when the invention hit the streets the world would never be the same.

I sometimes think about the rare brain—compared to my blonde brain—who could make all of this happen in such a short amount of time. I believe that the secret came from Leo's background, which encompassed so many talents. He was conservative to the core, exact with his expectations of himself and others, while at the same time remarkably innovative and free-thinking.

Leo knew how to use a drafting table, design and solder electronic circuitry, do woodworking, metalworking, build a facility, file a patent, invite feedback from the customers, design a mass-production manufacturing line, attract and hire good people, and quickly get rid of anyone who was lazy! Leo would laugh at the notion of doing only one thing, and he was the first in the plant to put out a fire and fix a machine with his own hands. He had to do it himself—because he invented many of those machines.

One day, tragedy struck. A bunch of employees were fixing an amplifier. Of course, Leo was right in there with them. At one point, Leo climbed down on the ground and stuck his head into the speaker cabinet to check on the wiring. Without warning, one of the men flipped the "on" switch of the amplifier, and the speakers burst out with a deafeningly loud squealing sound. Both of Leo's eardrums were shattered. He told me that he could feel them just melt away. In an instant, Leo lost most of his hearing. It was a devastating loss for a man who already was going through life with one glass eye. Besides, he loved music, he loved musicians, and he loved his role in making instruments. Suddenly, Leo's world was nearly silenced.

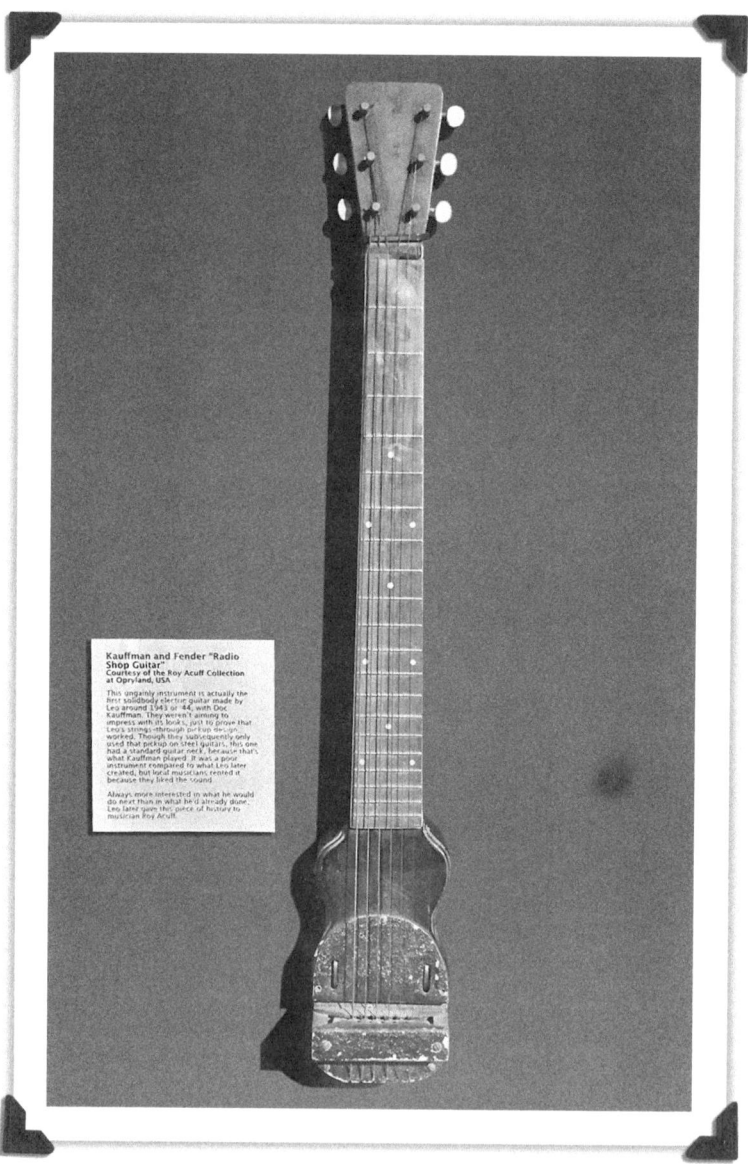

Leo invented this first solid body electric guitar

Later, Leo would get hearing aids, which greatly helped. Remarkably, even with these physical limitations, Leo never complained or made any kind of fuss about any of it. He simply did what Leo always did—he calmly went forward with a slight smile. His disabilities went virtually unnoticed by all the people around him.

Few would guess that Leo was a team player. At one point, he employed over a thousand people. His core team included not only Freddie Tavares, but also George Fullerton (no relation to the City of Fullerton) and Dale Hyatt.

Born in Arkansas, George Fullerton moved to Southern California in 1940 to work as a machinist. Leo hired George in 1948, and George worked with him until the day Leo passed away.

Dale Hyatt was a charismatic guy who oversaw the sales at Fender and was a longtime associate of Leo and George. Dale had been a tail gunner on a B-17 bomber who flew twenty-five missions and was once shot down over France. Dale began working for Leo in 1946. He left Fender Musical Instruments when Leo sold the business to CBS in 1965.

While never an official employee of Fender, Bob Perline was also a close friend of Leo's. Bob developed a popular advertising campaign that really grabbed people's attention. Bob said that when he drove from his home in Laguna Beach up to the Fender plant in Fullerton, he saw Freddie Tavares taking a break and hitting a tennis ball against the side of the building. The two chatted, and then Freddie said, "Well, let me introduce you to Leo."

Leo was keenly observant and could size people up rather quickly. Leo liked Bob and Bob liked Leo. They instantly hit it off, and Leo really loved the "You won't part with yours either" ad campaigns that Bob created because they were clever, really grabbed attention, and did not cost a lot of money! These were all winning qualities to Leo. Bob went around looking for people engaged in everyday activities, gave people a Fender guitar, and snapped pictures. He then cropped the photo and added the slogan. It was simple, yet powerful.

Bob was a classically trained, offbeat Laguna Beach artist, Mormon bishop, and beach bum, all wrapped into one. He took pictures of surfers playing a G-cord, (recruited on the spot near the Huntington

Beach pier), beautiful girls in bikinis with surfboards (friends of his daughters from Laguna Beach High School), smiling parachutists (hired on the spot before skydiving in Riverside), and a scuba diver (just some guy down at Crystal Cove) walking into the ocean, with a Fender guitar on his back. The whole thing was brilliant.

Leo loved these concepts, especially the ones with cute girls! I often teased Leo that the only thing that took his attention off guitars was a cute girl in tight jeans walking by!

While Leo was a quiet and subdued guy who often wore the same basic outfits, his head was always spinning with innovative ideas. His instruments were truly Southern California. Before Leo, there were no mint green or candy apple red musical instruments. Leo made them, along with glittery gold, turquoise blue, and shiny silver guitars. Fender guitars were fitting for jazz, country, and rock and roll. They were outrageous, but at the same time, they were solid, high-quality instruments, with a distinctive sound that everybody loved.

The most common question I get asked about Leo is, "What was he really like?" The truth is, no matter where he was or what he was doing, he was really thinking about musical instruments and amps. You could be talking with him for five minutes, and then in mid-conversation, he would get an idea and would just walk away. He would not say "excuse me" or "goodbye." He would just leave.

Because Leo was never in it for money or personal fame, he was an easy person to get behind and support, and his team greatly admired him. With Leo ever at the captain's wheel, this core team of Freddie, George, Dale, and Bob kept designing, inventing, producing, selling and promoting. The Telecaster, Stratocaster, and amplifiers grew and grew in popularity and eventually spread across the world.

Later, Leo got the idea to invent the electric bass guitar. The Fender bass turned music upside down, as up until then bass guitars were huge, fretless upright instruments. With Leo's invention, the bass player could run around the stage like everyone else. Without Leo, everyone from Gene Simmons to Sting would be plunking one of those huge, wooden basses on stage!

During this time *Guitar Player* magazine said,

> *Fender tube amps were enormously popular and set standards still followed by the industry; the competitors envied both their design and sales records. They sounded great, and they were hip – you could get a piggy-back (the father of the stack) with JBL's 30 years ago. To this day, even metal head Marshall Maniacs rave about the tonal hugeness of a small Fender amp cranked to tube meltdown. Nothing succeeds like success, and when it came to promotion, Fender's touch was solid gold. Ventures album covers looked like Fender ads; in a sense, they were. The Hendrix association still sells Strat's by the truckload, and the company continues to reap incalculable benefits from millions of fans seeing Fenders in the hands of everyone from Buddy Holly and Dick Dale to Beck, Richard and Clapton."*

For many years, Leo's life was a cycle of eating and sleeping in his modest home, driving a few blocks to the plant, where he would spend time quietly in his laboratory designing new instruments. Leo would also go out to the production line and check on how things were going, make executive decisions with regards to marketing and sales, go home, and then do it all again the next day.

However, this rigorous daily grind eventually got to be too much for Leo, and he became sickly and tired. Most people did not know it, but Leo had gotten a severe staph infection. It lingered and lingered and eventually got worse. The doctors told Leo that this was incurable and that he was going to die, so, in 1965, Leo decided to sell the company he had built. He wanted to wrap up his affairs so that when he died his wife, Esther, would not have to deal with them.

Guitar Player magazine explained this time well,

> *Don Randall, President of Fender Sales for years and later founder of Randall Instruments, was Fender's sole negotiator for the sale to CBS. Randall and CBS started negotiations in late August or September of 1964 and completed the deal, to be effective on January*

5th, 1965. "Of course, I consulted with Leo during the negotiations,"
recalled Don, "but basically, he had little or nothing to do with the
sale. He said, 'If I'm going to be rid of the company, I want to be rid
of it, period. I'm leaving it up to you.' Leo wouldn't even go back to
New York and pick up his check. I picked up his share of the booty
and deposited it for him. He was busy working at Fender."

Publicly, Leo told people that he had no regrets selling Fender to
CBS. He even went so far as to complain about locking all the doors at
night and about the electrical outages. Leo told *Guitar Player* magazine,
"I wouldn't want the company back now as a gift. It was just too much,
too much trouble."

Leo and Esther's Fullerton home

Yet privately, Leo felt quite differently. Leo only sold the company
because of the staph infection, believing he was going to die. Later,
he met another doctor in Anaheim who injected him with two large

shots containing very high levels of antibiotics. Leo said it was the largest syringe he had ever seen. That alone almost killed him, and the treatments left Leo feeling very weak and sick, but soon he was completely cured! However, by this time the sale was a done deal, and the agreement included a non-compete clause, which prohibited Leo from creating a new company for ten years. Although Leo remained at Fender for many years as a consultant, he told me many times that he regretted the sale.

Leo and Esther in Egypt

Nevertheless, Fender Musical Instruments really exploded in the Raymond Building, where Leo continued to consult for many years. That ugly, concrete building was the epicenter of the Fender revolution.

In 1985, after making history on Raymond Avenue in Fullerton for thirty-two years, the Fender plant moved. Pete Bell, who had headed up the research and development team for Fender, walked all alone through the facilities for the last time. He checked each room and turned off all the lights, locked the door, and put the keys in the mail slot. We can only guess what Pete was thinking about. Fender was interwoven into his life and his community. Perhaps he thought about the friends he had made, like the guy who painted all the guitars and then took time on the weekend to paint his daughter's car. Perhaps he recalled the time when Freddie Tavares and his wife played the guitar at his daughter's wedding.

A young Leo, so full of energy!

Maybe Pete was thinking about the days he spent with Eric Clapton talking about his guitar, with Carl Palmer discussing his drums, or with the hundreds of other musicians he had met over the years. True to the Fender culture, he had no photos and no autographs—just great memories. It was like a big fun family, and now that wonderful era was over.

However, Pete did keep one thing. All the old tables, furniture, and workbenches were being thrown out and were sitting out in the yard area. He took home his favorite, old military-green workbench from the research and development department. The Telecaster and Stratocaster were invented on that bench. That bench now sits on display at the Fullerton Museum Center.

Pete got in his car and drove to his home just a few streets from where Leo lived, now retired from his favorite job. That Fullerton chapter of Fender had now closed for good, but other chapters were just opening. Fender Musical Instruments moved to Corona and Mexico, while Leo created G&L with George Fullerton. In establishing G&L, Leo remained loyal to Fullerton and established his new factory down the street from the original site on Fender Avenue.

The work of Leo rolled on.

CHAPTER 4

A New Era

I n 1979, Leo's wife, Esther, passed away after a long battle with lung cancer. I had never met Leo or Esther before she died, but, from all accounts, she was a lovely person. People that knew her well always said that she was wonderful and very outgoing. In the few pictures that I have seen of her over the years, she was laughing.

Sadly, Esther got lung cancer at the Pacific Bell phone company, where she worked as an operator at a time when people smoked indoors. Neither Esther nor Leo were smokers, but she inhaled a lot of second-hand smoke at work.

For years, I had known George and Lucille Fullerton from church. In fact, our families had started Temple Baptist Church together under an apricot tree in my parent's backyard, and it eventually grew into a free-standing church, with a large congregation on Malvern Avenue in Fullerton.

Esther and Leo had first lived in a one-bedroom, one-bath duplex near Harbor Boulevard. When the Raymond Avenue plant opened, they moved to a modest, three-bedroom tract house near the plant, where they lived for many years. However, when Esther became ill, they both felt that it was easier for her to get around in a small mobile home, rather than a full-sized house. Also, Esther's sister-in-law lived in the same mobile home park, so she could help take care of her when Leo was at work. Leo made all the arrangements, and they lived there until Esther passed away.

Leo and Esther had no children, and with Esther now gone, George and Lucille noticed that Leo was getting lonely. There was no one at home for Leo to be with, have a meal with or even spend any time with outside of work. So, George and Lucille were kind to Leo and invited him over to their house for dinner three or four times a week. Leo would eat dinner and then go back to his mobile home where he would go right back to working. The only close relative Leo had was his sister, Wilda, who lived in Anaheim. However, they only got together at Christmas.

The Fullerton's became concerned about Leo because he seemed to be in a lingering state of sadness and even a bit of a depression. Leo had gotten the best medical attention for Esther that money could buy, but still felt guilty because he felt he had not taken enough time to be with her during her illness. Leo had other people take her to Mexico and Arizona, and other doctors here and there, all trying to find a cure.

Lucille Fullerton and I had been best friends for many years. One day Lucille said, "You know you're writing those funny stories about 'Parents Without Partners.' Could I show a few to Leo?" My messages were about how we are all responsible for our own happiness, and how we cannot expect our kids, dogs, church, or anybody else to make us happy. I would write, "You make yourself happy!"

Lucille showed them to Leo. She said he really enjoyed them because they were silly. She once asked me, "Do you think some day you could come by and meet Leo? Just pretend like you are stopping by to purchase some of my Mary Kay products, and I'll introduce you, and maybe you could just talk to him, and cheer him up!"

So that is just what I did. One night after dinner, I went over to their home and pretended to buy some Mary Kay lipstick. When Leo had finished eating, we all went to the den. George and Lucille walked in the den first, and Leo followed and sat in the big chair. I sat on the ottoman next to him. I was thinking that they would sit down by us, but they quickly turned around and said they would talk to us after a while, and then left the room!

I had never met this man before! I did not know a single thing about him. I didn't know anything about the music industry. I was just talking to a stranger, but I do love to talk! We started talking, and he immediately started talking about Esther.

He said he had read what I wrote. "I don't know if I can make myself happy," he said.

"It's only been a year," I said. "There's time. You will be." He started to weep. The tears were rolling down. We talked, and we talked. He wept for quite a while. I came over to the house and talked to him three or four different times, and each time was easier. He got to know me. I got to know him.

Lucille called me one day, and she said, "You've met Leo. Now he's comfortable with you. Why don't you come over for dinner?"

"Okay," I said. "That's fine. I like a free dinner!"

"Just understand that when Leo's having dinner that's all he thinks about—eating. If he doesn't talk to you, it's not that he's being rude. It's just he likes to eat."

I just laughed and said, "That's fine with me. I'll talk to you guys."

We sat down, and they were at one end of the table. Leo and I were at the other end. Leo had said a few words to me when I sat down, and I saw George at the other end of the table just laughing. Leo was telling me these things, and they were laughing and laughing.

I asked, "What are you guys laughing about?"

"If we knew all we had to do was put a blonde next to him to get him to talk, we'd have done it months ago!" Leo heard them say that, and we all just laughed. We all continued sitting around the table kidding around, talking and laughing. It was a lot of fun.

A few weeks later, Leo had gotten an invitation to go to a Country Music Association's Christmas party at the Palomino Club in Los Angeles. Leo called Lucille and asked, "Do you think Phyllis would like to go?"

Lucille said, "Well, Leo, that would be considered a date. You have to ask her."

He said, "No, I can't…I can't. You're her friend. You ask her."

"No," she replied. "I'm not going to! If you want her to go with you, then you have to call her!"

THE CALL

One December day in 1979, the phone rang, and I picked it up. There was no caller ID in those days. There was no text or email to set up an appointment to call. Today a phone call can get complicated, but, in those days, you just picked up the phone and called.

"Hi, Phyllis. It's Leo." He just sort of stumbled around.

I said, "Oh, hi Leo. How you doin'? Whatcha doin'? Are you at work?" We were kind of just chitchatting.

He was mumbling, but he was not really saying anything. Then Leo just blurted out, "George and Lucille and I are going to a Christmas party. Do you want to come?"

I was so surprised. "Where—where is this going to be?"

"In Los Angeles," he replied.

He also said George was going to drive. I was very glad for that. I was hoping Leo was not going to drive. I had driven with him before, and it was a near-death experience. So, we went on our first date. Of course, we had fun, and Leo just kept calling and calling, and I kept picking up the phone!

A TIME TO HUG

It is so sad to say, but prior to me, Leo had never had a hug in his entire life. Leo's German Mom was somewhat stern, and while Esther was a wonderful woman, she was simply not a hugger. Leo had gone through his life 100% hugless.

On the other hand, I am not only a hugger, but I practically have a black belt in hugging. I was trained by the best! My big family are all huggers. I have always felt so blessed to have this huge, wonderful family that just loves to be together, eat and tell stories. We just love each other. Our family hugs dogs, cats, trees—whatever. Whoever came through the door got a hug from everyone else. Hugging was just a part of the landscape in my family and considered an essential life skill!

When Leo and I first started dating, I did what I always do. I gave him a hug. But Leo immediately went into shock! He kind of went rigid and nervously backed up. Maybe he thought that we were going to wrestle or something. This was a complete alien encounter for him! I immediately and matter-of-factly told him, "Now Leo, if I am going to stick around, you are going to get a hug." I would tease him, "And if you run, I can catch you!" He was really stunned, it was hilarious!

Of course, I do not take "no" for an answer, and I just kept hugging him. Deep down, he knew he liked it because he just kept calling and calling. Gradually he went from being freaked out to simply standing there to accept the inevitable. As more time went by, Leo made token attempts to sort of hug back. First with one arm, and later with two arms. It was feeling kinda good! This was real progress.

After a while, Leo became a certified hugger! Whenever we met, I was so happy to see him, and he was happy to see me, and we eventually had big hugs. The impossible had become a reality! Miracles do exist, and the proof is that Leo became a legitimate, true-blue hugger.

After a while, whenever Leo arrived he would come through the door, stand there with his hands on his hips, and loudly demand, "Where's my hug!?!" And he really meant it. He wanted that hug, and he wanted it now! And of course, he always got it, and he and I would just hug and smile!

THE PROPOSAL

Leo and I had been seeing each other for several months. I do not know if either one of us ever thought about getting married because he was older than I was. We both had our lives, and it was not a *necessity* to get married. We had enjoyed spending time together, and it sounded like fun.

One night in June of 1980, Leo and I were sitting at the table of a Mexican restaurant at the Tustin shopping mall enjoying some great food.

Leo said, "I suppose people think we should get married,"

"I've heard a few people mention that."

"Well," he said, "It won't be fair to you because I'm a lot older than you."

"Leo," I said, "that's okay with me."

Leo just kept eating and eating—it felt like forever. Finally, he put his fork down, looked at me and he said, "I guess then we ought to get married then."

"Ok," I said, "we need to go tell my folks."

Even though I was in my 40s at the time, I was still really close to my parents, so I wanted to get their approval. We went to my parents' house. Mom had cookies out on the table. We were eating them, and they were looking at us as if to say, "Why are you here?" They knew me well enough to know that something was up.

"Well," I said, "Leo and I have decided to get married." My mother walked up to Leo, pushed her pointed finger against his chest, and said, "I don't mind if you marry my daughter, but don't you ever call me 'Mom.'" Leo laughed. She laughed, too, but she was serious at the same time. Occasionally over the years, he would say, "Okay, Mom," and she would glare at him, but only in fun.

The next day we went down to a jewelry store and bought a ring. Leo had told me in the months before we decided to get married that he felt guilty he had not purchased Esther, the first Mrs. Fender, much jewelry. She really, really liked jewelry.

"So," Leo said. "I want to get you a really nice ring."

"No, Leo," I said. "All I want is a gold band. I really, really just want a gold band." We went to the jewelers' and he was showing us all kinds of diamond rings.

I said, "Leo, I just want a gold band."

"Phyllis," he said, "you have to understand you're going to be Mrs.

Fender, and everybody's going to expect Mrs. Fender to have a big diamond ring."

"But Leo I'm—I'm not fancy. I want a gold band, 'cause I've been married before."

"Well," he said, "I'll pick one. I'll pick something out for you."

The man at the counter came back with this beautiful diamond ring. It was a band ring, and it had thirty-two little diamonds in it. I said, "Leo, it is beautiful. It really is beautiful, but I just want a gold band." He said, "You can put the gold band under this one." That is exactly what I did.

This ring he chose is beautiful. It has lots and lots of little diamonds, and beautiful scalloped edges. Leo was always so proud that he had bought that for me. He said, "Mrs. Fender needs to have the diamonds." I did not feel like Mrs. Fender in the beginning. I was just Phyllis. But he was proud of the ring. He was very, very proud. So, he won that argument, and we both left smiling!

Our Wedding!

OUR WEDDING NIGHT

On September 20, 1980, Leo and I were married on the Love Boat, the actual ship that was used for the 1970s television show. We had both our wedding and reception there on the ship. It was fun. There was a short, beautiful ceremony, dinner, and a sweet little cake. My favorite part was when Freddie and Tamar Tavares played beautiful music on a guitar that he and Leo had invented. Freddie could have played any guitar in the world he wanted, yet he always chose a white, Fender Jaguar with a rosewood neck and a tortoise shell pickguard—and, boy, could he make that guitar sing! Freddie was the real deal, and both Leo and I adored him and his wonderful wife. Their music made our wedding extra special.

The feeling was mutual, Freddie once told *Guitar Player* magazine:

It's difficult to overstate Mr. Fender's impact on his industry. He changed it, revolutionized it, and turned it upside down. He altered the look, the sound and the personality of American music, yet it would be hard to imagine a man of plainer appearance or fewer affectations. He never wore any kind of clothes that you'd expect a person in his position to wear. People didn't have the slightest idea that he was any kind of a wheel. Leo never flew off the handle, never raised his voice. With all his stresses and strains, he still tried to keep everyone's spirits up.

We had such a good time with a small group of family and friends. When the party ended, Leo and I went back to the cabin. Leo said he was going to go into the bathroom first. I waited for my turn.

I went to the sink to brush my teeth and saw this little black box next to the water faucet. I thought to myself, "Somebody told Leo to buy a present for his new bride," I wondered to myself, "Oh, should I open it now? Or should I take it out into the bedroom and share the moment with Leo?"

I looked down at the box. I thought to myself, "I can't stand it. I'm going to open it now!" I opened that beautiful little black box. It was not a ring or a necklace or a bracelet or any other beautiful piece of jewelry—it was a glass eye! It was beautiful, but it was not something I could wear! I was in such shock, so, I closed it up, turned the light off, and took the little black box with me.

"I saw a little black box in there by the sink," I told Leo.

"Yeah" he responded.

"And I opened it." I replied.

Leo and I enjoying our wedding cake

"Oh, yeah?" responded Leo. "That's my eye."

"What?!"

"Yeah," he said without any hesitation, "I've had a glass eye since I was seven years old."

I had no idea! I would have never, ever, ever guessed. It was the most beautiful, baby blue eye! It could almost be jewelry. He surprised me not with a wedding present, but with an eyeball. We had to carry the little glass eye with us everywhere that we went. But you would never know, and most never did know that he had a glass eye. Now it can be our little secret!

A NEW HOME

Out of the blue, one day Leo said, "You know, we've got to get a house." Leo always thought things over before he said anything, and he of course had a clear plan. He declared, "This is what I want, and I don't want it any other way. I want a house ten minutes from my plant because I don't want to be driving all over town, wasting work time!"

I would come home from church every Sunday, change my clothes, and get my dog. I would then drive around all the neighborhoods that were about ten minutes away from the plant. Whenever I saw an "open house" sign, I would go in, and walk around the house, and ask myself, "Okay, now would Leo like this? Would I like this? Would it be large enough for our family?"

When Leo and I got married, he got a big, built-in family. He and his sister were the only children in his family. Esther and he had no children, and they were not very close to the rest of his family.

When Leo met me, he thought it was unusual to have all these people around, all the time. We're a very close family. So, the day that he married me on the Love Boat he got a wife, a mother-in-law, a father-in-law, three kids, and one beautiful baby granddaughter. Suddenly, Leo was a stepfather to three kids and a grandpa to baby Stefani! All in one evening on the Love Boat. We always laughed that he gave me the music industry, and I gave him a big, close family.

Leo and I enjoyed our three beautiful children. Our oldest son was Paul, and Leo loved to just sit and talk and talk with him. Paul has always been the solid voice of reason in the room. The second was our classically beautiful daughter, Chris, whom Leo would just admire and quietly visit with. The third was Jon, who is the family comic and made Leo laugh and laugh.

We needed a house that would accommodate us all. As I searched for houses, I would just put the address down in a small notebook. I did that for several weeks, and then I gave the list to Leo, who gave it to a real estate agent he was working with. That was the last I heard of the house for a while.

Leo and I were out to eat at Polly's Pies on Raymond Avenue, just up the street from the Fender plant. It seems like a lot of the fun things happen when we are out to eat.

I asked, "Anything interesting happened at the plant today?"

"No, not really," Leo said. "Just—just plain old stuff."

"Well did anybody important come in?"

"No," he said. "Just people."

"Oh, you wasted the whole day?" I teased.

And he went, "Well, I guess—I guess it was okay."

I started to ask, "What did you—"

"I bought us a house." He said very calmly.

"What?! What?!"

"Yeah, one of those off your list."

"Which one? Which one?" I could hardly breath with anticipation.

Leo answered, "The house right here, the fourth one on your list." I burst out crying in the middle of the restaurant. Everybody turned around to see what this man was doing to this wonderful woman to make her cry! I was bawling. He reached over, grabbed my arm, and said, "You didn't like that one?"

"It was my favorite!" I said through my sobs, "It was my favorite!"

"Are you sure?"

"It was my favorite!" I grabbed his arm, and I said, "Come on we're going—we're going to see the house.

"I'm not finished eating!" Leo said.

"I don't care," I said bawling. "We're going to go see the house."

Leo hated missing an opportunity to eat, but he grudgingly got up. We got into the car and drove out to our new house. We sat for about two hours in front and talked about our new house and when we could move in.

As we were not yet married, I moved into the big, beautiful home by myself. It was July, and we were not getting married until September. In the meantime, all I had was a card table, two folding chairs, plus a metal chaise lounge chair, like the ones out by a swimming pool. That metal chaise chair was my bed until we got married.

While we were on our honeymoon, my family moved my furniture into the house, while the guys from the plant moved in all of Leo's furniture. As I have told that story over the years, people have asked why my family did not just move in my furniture, when I moved into the house in July. Until this day I have no idea. I just never thought to ask.

For a man of Leo's fame and fortune, our home was quite modest. People imagine something bigger and more lavish, but for us it was perfect. It is a classic old Fullerton ranch style home, but I love that it has a wonderful view of Orange Country and a beautiful pool. Leo often enjoyed the view, but I saw him swim in our pool exactly once. My sister Laurie teased and teased him about not being able to swim. Finally, Leo had enough. He got in the shallow end, swam to the deep end and back, and got out. He proved he could swim, and that was the only time Leo got into the pool!

Freddie and Tamar Tavares

Life was wonderful in our new home. Leo had a home office, where he would disappear for hours on end. There were times when I'd say, "Gee, you know Leo, I really would like to go down to the beach and watch the sunset. Can we go?" And he would say, "No.

I've got to finish this drawing." I would be a little disappointed, as I actually wanted him to enjoy the sunset. However, if he knew the kids were coming over or if my mother was bringing food, he would get excited and drop his work. Over the years, we had countless hours of work, meals, get-togethers, and fun in our home!

CHAPTER 5

Leo at Home

PRIVATE LIFE

Leo was famously quiet, and he was also quite private. In all our years together, we never had a single worker in our house. He rarely spoke to the neighbors, except to just quickly chat, or say, "Hello."

If something in the house broke, like a heater or plumbing, Leo would take care of it himself. He would climb around, check it out, go down to the hardware store, buy parts, and just fix it himself. As far as the cooking or cleaning, Leo considered it out of the question to hire someone to do it. I not only worked full-time myself, but I also cooked all the meals, and cleaned the whole house.

You can take that image of the world-famous inventor, surrounded by maids and butlers, and just throw it out the window. Leo could afford all that, but he did not want the fuss. Leo did not want anyone coming into our home, except for friends and family.

The construction of Leo's mobile home

THE MORNING ROUTINE

Leo got up each morning around six. He would get out of bed, go into the bathroom, and fill the tub up with very hot water. Then he would sit, and soak in the tub for about an hour. This was his personal time for meditation, thinking, and quiet reflection. Sometimes he would doze off a bit. The hot bath was his morning ritual.

After his meditative bath, Leo always told me he did not want to waste time trying to decide what to wear every day. He simply wanted to get to work!

So, every day of his life, Leo chose between a selection of black pants, black shoes, black socks, and black belts. His only choice was between a white or baby blue short-sleeve shirt. There were only a few, rare deviations from this routine. He did not like suits and ties. He had a snap-on tie when he had to wear it, but he snapped it back off the second he could.

Other choices simply depended on the weather. If it was cold, he wore a black windbreaker. If it was warm, he would just have a short-sleeved shirt. If it was very cold, he had something a little heavier than a windbreaker, but it also was black.

Leo's sleepwear was a black sweat suit, with black socks. He did not have to think about fashion a lot. This fashion routine made it easy to pack for trips, and no time was wasted about worrying about what to wear.

Leo and Granddaughter Jessica, playing with her Easter bonnet

He always wore a short-sleeve shirt with breast pockets. In the pocket was a white, plastic pocket protector, and in this little holder was a pencil, pen, little notebook, small ruler, and tiny screwdriver that would fit into a guitar. He always kept this with him, except when he slept! Leo did not care if anyone liked it or not. That was him.

After his bath and getting dressed, he would make healthy carrot juice. Once in a while, he added bacon. I would just watch and smile. That was my Leo. He was one of a kind!

LEO AND PETS

Leo and my father, Bill Dalton, were both eccentric men, but in different ways, and I think they were both intrigued with each other.

Dad always loved pets, all kinds of pets, and it was not uncommon for him to have a parrot on his shoulder when he ate. Dad could not resist giving dogs a tickle. We had all kinds of pets at our house.

Leo was always amazed at the things people did. Like the parrot, church, family dinners, or having a lot of kids around—there were so many things about my family that were so far from his range of experiences.

Leo came off like an unapproachable Wizard of Oz. Most would not dare approach the man behind the curtain! But at home, at the dinner table, Leo would love to chat about China's Great Wall, its surrounding cities or villages, or going up and down the Amazon River, and how dark the water was. I can just see him sitting there, feeding the dogs scraps under the table. I remember him playing with the puppies. He was such a gentle man with the little dogs. He was just like you and me—just a real, simple person. At heart, Leo was just a farm boy with simple values.

Before we got married, I had a dog that was quite ugly. I called her Curly Dog because I wanted her to think she was pretty. One day, I was driving down the street somewhere in Fullerton, and she was on my lap looking out the window. A car pulled up beside me and beeped the horn. I thought, "Well, maybe I have a flat tire or something." I finally rolled down the window, and they said, "That's the ugliest dog I ever saw in the whole world!" I quickly covered up her ears, so she would not hear!

Leo getting whistling lessons from my sister Laurie and friend Theo

I admit that she was not beautiful, but she was one of the best dogs I have ever had. She went to work with me. She used to sleep under my desk. She would just lay there. She would wander off to Dad's office at times, and she knew which drawer Dad kept his chocolates in. She would go in there, whether Dad had a client or not, and sat there with her nose on the chocolate drawer. She would just stand there until Dad opened it and gave her a small bite.

Leo always liked dogs, and he ended up falling in love with my Curly Dog. He would tickle her, or whatever dog was around, just like Dad did. Since Curly Dog, I have gotten mostly Chihuahuas. Not teeny-tiny ones, but small ones. Now my Chihuahua is so big, that I call her a miniature pot-bellied pig. She may be a tad overweight, but I do not tell her that.

THE WILLIE NELSON ARGUMENT

Leo and I enjoyed a wonderful life together and, most of the time we had so much fun! But from time to time we had our little differences, just like anyone else. But looking back, we did not take things too seriously, we just laughed about it all.

Our first argument was over another man, Willie Nelson! He is still one of my favorite singers. I have always wanted to meet Willie Nelson! I always dreamed of the day when Willie would come by the plant, and Leo would call me. Then I could come down and say, "Hello!"

We were talking about something or other, and a Willie Nelson song came on the radio. I teasingly said, "Boy, I wished you could make a guitar that sounded like Willie Nelson's." I said, "If you could make a guitar that sounded like that, you might *really* be famous!"

Leo was not amused at all. Leo never yelled or anything like that. He looked at me sternly and said, "That's not funny." Then he walked into the other room, and I did not see him again until the next day!

GIRLS AND GUITARS

Leo thought it was wonderful when girls learned to play the guitar. One day, I thought that I might want to learn how to play.

I do not have Leo's brains. I have blonde brains. However, I love the look of pretty fingernails! So, I asked, "Hey Leo, I would really love to learn how to play the guitar. You are so smart and clever. Can you invent one that I can play without cutting my nails?"

Leo just kind of sat and looked at me, in the Leo kinda way. He had a way of just getting right to the point, and he said, "Look Phyllis, you have two choices, and only two choices. You can play the guitar, or you can have long fingernails. What's it gonna be?"

Well, that settled it. I never learned how to play the guitar, but I still have my long fingernails!

Leo sharing a new guitar with my sister Laurie

LEO AND MONEY

Even though Leo had a lot of money, you would never know it. At restaurants, Leo was a cheap tipper. He would put down a dollar regardless of the total on the bill, and then, as we left, I would put a five-dollar bill on top of it. I was once a waitress, and former waitresses always make good tippers, because we know how hard the work is!

Leo was quite careful with his money, and he rarely talked about it. When Leo and I were married I kept my job, so I was still earning an income. Once a month he would give me a household check. It was for me to take care of the bills, buy groceries, and manage the house.

Once in a while, I would go over my budget. I would go down to his secretary and say, "You know, I could use a couple more dollars." She said, "You know, that's up to Leo." A lot of times he said, "No." I said, "Well yeah, Christmas is coming."

At Christmas, Leo would watch the kids and grandkids open their presents, and then go back to work. He told me, "Well, you don't need to buy so many presents." I would reply, "I cannot help it. I love to buy a lot of presents, and we have a lot of family."

I did not get upset because I was still working, and I got to keep my pay check. The household check was for the household. I used my check for play money. I am glad I had kept working, and had my own paycheck to play "Santa" with!

For being a little tight with money, Leo did some good charity work. He and Esther's names are on one of the cardiac care suites at St. Jude Hospital in Fullerton. He donated to the YMCA. He was very generous to them.

When I developed a heart problem, I said, "Wouldn't it be interesting if they put me in Leo and Esther's room at the hospital." In fact, when I was taken to the cardiac area, they asked me my name, and I responded, "Phyllis Fender."

They just kind of looked at me and said, "Don't you have a room here?"

"That was my husband and the other Mrs. Fender."

"Oh," they said, "we just wanted to be sure you got in the right room if that was your room."

"No," I said, "that was before my time."

When we flew, Leo and I always travelled in coach. Leo's attitude was that you are going to get to your destination at the same time, no matter where you sit on the plane! And, as usual, Leo was right!

Leo was not much of a shopper. Once in a while, he might swing big, and pick up a bag of apples or something. Shopping was my job. I was the lady of the house, and that is what my monthly household check was for.

Leo did buy his own clothes, which was easy. He just went into J.C. Penny's, or someplace like that, and bought anything black. If we went to the drugstore or supermarket, he said, "Okay, I'm going to go over here." And he would just take off. I would come back, see him in the checkout line, and I would say, "Leo, I'm not finished." He would just wave, and stand there by the exit with his packages in his hand. He said, "Yes after you pay we'll go." He would expect me to pay for the things that I bought, and he only paid for what he bought.

Leo never threw money around; he was always careful. Whenever we shopped, he would always ask, "Are you sure you need that? Are you really sure you need it?" I would say, "No, I don't need it, but I want it!" This may sound awful, but it was easier and more fun to go shopping by myself!

THE PIANO ARGUMENT

With money, normally I would stick to my budget, and there was no problem. But one day Leo and I had a big blowup over a piano. When you walked into our house, you felt at home.

We have a forever view of Fullerton and Orange County. There is a corner of the living room that was just crying out for a beautiful baby grand piano.

One day I told Leo, "I really would like to buy a piano for this corner. I want it to look like a piece of furniture, we could put a flower pot on."

"No," he said.

"You don't want us to have a piano?" I asked.

"No," he said, "but—that's not the kind you're going to get."

"Well, what kind?" I inquired, now I was curious.

And then he said, "Well, I'm…I'm making a stand for it … down at the shop."

"No," I said. "I don't think so."

I knew Leo was thinking of one of those black vinyl stage Rhodes pianos that bands like KISS or Aerosmith used for their concerts. I thought, "You have to be kidding!" I suppose he wanted strobe lights and groupies to go with it! The whole idea was ridiculous!

"Well," Leo said, "we're going to get a Fender Rhodes piano."

"They're ugly." I quickly responded.

He said, "That doesn't matter. They still sound good."

"No, Leo, this is going to be furniture. It's going to be a wooden piano sitting in here with a flower arrangement on it."

He insisted, "We're going to put it over here." He meant where he had had his stereo and all his equipment.

"No, but it's black metal." I said again, "It's ugly!"

"Well, it's got a lot of tunes on it. You can play all kinds of stuff." He kept trying to convince me.

"Leo, it's *ugly*." I insisted.

He was really upset with me. He said, "Well," he said, "then I'm not buying it for you."

I announced, "Okay then, I'll just buy it for myself."

And I did. I was still working at my family's company, and it took three years to pay for it. But I bought it myself, and it's still beautiful!

FAVORITE TV SHOW

Leo was not crazy about television. If we ever happened to be watching TV together, we would probably watch cowboy shows or the news. By far his favorite TV show was *Gunsmoke*.

In particular, he liked the character "Doc" because, he said, "Doc cares about people, and he's trying to help everyone out." He went on, "I like him because he is always there for others. He cares what happens to these people. The other people are shootin' at each other and doing all this kind of stuff, but Doc was always honest, true, and helping others."

That was interesting because Leo was pretty much describing himself. Here is this crazy world with nutty politics, wars, poverty, and everything else. Then there is Leo, just quietly building the instruments that create music, that make the world a nicer place.

LEO AND DAD

Leo and Dad, Bill, had a good relationship. Dad had been successful in the bakery and restaurant business. I worked for my father for twenty-two years as the vice president of Dalton's Bakery

Equipment. My grandfather started the business and designed large-scale commercial revolving ovens in 1917 in Los Angeles. He kept it going until just about 1938 or 1940. My grandfather passed away when I was in the sixth grade, so Dad took over the business.

Dad had been a baker for a while, and boy could he bake. Once he took over, he modernized the oven. Dad was well known in the baking industry, and he installed bakeries in Japan, Canada, Mexico, and Australia, as well as all over the United States.

Occasionally, I think that Leo was a bit jealous, not that my father was hugely financially successful, but because every customer wanted to be his friend. Dad remembered all his customers' names and gave them generous discounts.

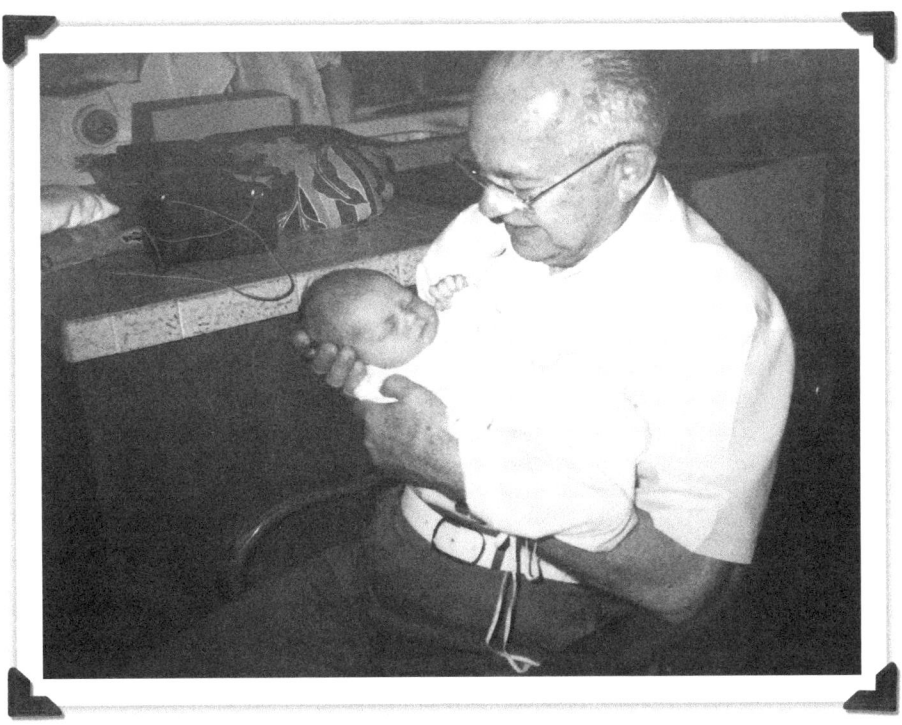

Leo loves his grandchildren!

On the other hand, Leo did not give a lot of discounts, and, honestly, he did not have a lot of friends outside of the music business.

It was not that he was unfriendly or that he did not want to know people. It was that people would take time away from work. Leo saw that my father was more of a people person. In the twenty-some years that I worked for my father, every customer became a friend. Leo closely watched my father at family parties and get-togethers. He saw this smiling, lovely man, who was larger than life, interacting with everybody.

Leo would ask me, "How does your Dad have time to work?" He did not understand that, in sales, it helps to be friendly. If he had just been working for money, he would not have been as successful. My father was very much a gentleman.

Sometimes I thought Leo was a little sad that he never had that kind of friendship with others. But again, he never wanted to take the time. Leo's customers were happy and committed enough, and there was certainly a lot of respect both ways, but I think Leo envied how easily my father developed friendships. Leo was fascinated by this tender, caring business man.

Leo's time was measured in what he was creating. There were days that I hardly even saw him because he was so driven to get a project finished. Whereas Dad always played with the family, was active at the church, went to every one of his grandkids' sporting events, and just loved everyone he met. Dad was the original "Mr. Sportsman" and "Mr. Baker" and "Mr. Everyone's Friend" and all this kind of stuff. He and Leo really did not have a lot to talk about, other than both being business owners.

Leo and my father related well as far as business went, as they both liked to continually improve products for their customers. Dad was not a great businessman. He was never about making a lot of money, but he was a great one to do business *with*. He would give his customers the best price. We would say, "Dad, you have to charge more than five percent profit! Five percent is not going to pay the rent." And he would quickly respond, "But they'll come back happy!" Dad always did just what he wanted to do—just like Leo!

WHITE CARS

Leo had read a report, or heard something on TV, that said that white cars were best, because they were easier to see and therefore safer. Leo had this notion permanently imbedded in his brain, and he had a missionary zeal about it.

Leo, me and Curly Dog at Christmas 1982

Leo got both of us white cars after we were married. Everybody in his office then was required to have a white car. He was convinced that the world would be a better place if everyone drove a white car.

"But what if it's foggy?" I asked. "They'd be harder to see."

"No," he insisted. "Somehow the other cars would see them."

"Yeah," I said. "But they would see your red car even better in the fog."

"No," he said. "Only white cars are safe."

There was no changing his mind. So, he and everybody around him had white cars. That is until I told Leo that I loved blue Cadillacs, and then, all of a sudden, my white Lincoln turned into a Dodger blue Cadillac!

The way he got my new car was not romantic. We just went down to the Cadillac dealership together one day, shortly after I made my comment about wanting a Dodger blue Cadillac. He did the paperwork to buy it, and then he drove off to work. I sat by myself waiting for the car to get fixed up and ready to take home. There was no fanfare with Leo.

One day, I drove my new blue car down to the plant to give Leo some information. I pulled up in front, and some of the employees were outside having lunch.

They kept asking, "How come you have a blue car?"

"Well, it's a present from Leo. It's a Christmas present and a birthday present from Leo."

They asked, "But how come you don't have a white car?"

"Because I look better in blue!"

They were really upset and said, "He made us all buy white cars."

"Well," I answered, "I hug better than you do."

"But that's not fair."

"You're going to have to tell him that," I said, as I drove off with a smile, blowing them a kiss.

Leo's thing for white cars was funny because it was based in his belief that they were safer. Yet Leo's driving was anything but safe, it was horrible. Let's just say that Jesus and I had many, many conversations every time he got behind the wheel! The only good thing I can say about his driving, was that he was slooooooow.

Everybody else always had white cars until the very end of Leo's life. My beautiful Dodger blue car was stolen one day about twenty years ago while I was having my nails done, and we never found a trace of it. But I still look for it whenever I am driving around Fullerton. I loved that car and never saw another one like it.

CHAPTER 6

Leo's Diet and Exercise

BACON LOVE

Leo's diet and exercise routine was simple—he never dieted and he never exercised. The only time I hated Leo, was when I watched him eat and eat, and not gain a pound!

This man loved to eat, yet remarkably he was never overweight. This inspired him to eat even more! Let's just say that life with Leo was interesting. There was an endless list of things that Leo did that were odd. Leo may have invented the electric guitar, but he also invented deep-fried bacon. Really!

When Leo took people out on his boat, he loved to cook breakfast for everybody. He would get up early and cook bacon. By cooking bacon, I mean he took a frying pan and filled it about half-full of cooking oil, heated it up, lay down the bacon, and let it sizzle and sizzle. I honestly have never seen anything like it. It was so hard and greasy, but he proudly served it up!

"You know it's kind of hard," I would say when he would cook at home, "It's got an awful lot of oil in it. How about we just kind of fry it nicely over here in a pan?" Pointing to a pan with no oil in it.

"No, no—it has to be this way." He would insist.

"But Leo, you're getting so much oil on the bacon."

"That's the way I like it," he would say. "Nobody on the boat ever complained."

Leo loved getting a senior discount at Sizzler

"Well," I said, "I'm not complaining, it's just that an awful lot of oil."

Leo would just say, "Well that's the way I like to cook it. So, if we're going to have breakfast, we're going to have it this way."

Leo was the boss. Whatever he was doing, he was set on doing it his way, whether it was white cars, carrot juice machines, or bacon in a sea of oil. That's the way it was always done. "That's alright," I would say. "I'll eat some cantaloupe, and you can eat your deep-fried bacon."

Leo did not want to waste time learning something new, so he would do repetitive things. It almost sounds like an illness, but it was not. He always cooked his bacon a certain way, he wanted the laundry a certain way, he even had a certain order to line up the trash cans. He always had to take the cans down to the street so that he could put them in their proper order, and I had to put them back after they were emptied.

CHURCH POTLUCKS

While I attended church regularly, Leo did less so. He preferred to be out on his boat and would often spend the weekend on Catalina Island. Leo just could not concentrate enough to sit in church, so he did not go as much until later in his life.

The only exception was for the church potlucks! Leo was the first in line for a potluck. We always teased that Baptists do two things well. We know how to take collections and how to have good potlucks! My church was no exception.

At that time, our church had seven or eight hundred members, so a potluck was really something to behold. He was so excited because there were a lot of farm people, which meant there would be a lot of good old farm food. Leo went crazy for the pot roasts, and there was every kind of casserole you could imagine. And boy, he was he happy when he could just fill up his plate! Later in life when he had Parkinson's, you would never know it. He could still move fast at the potluck.

Leo was crazy about vegetables. He loved vegetables, and he enjoyed seeing this long table full of them, especially because he did not have to pay for it! Leo would always go back for seconds, and he always managed to find room for dessert!

There was a whole church full of people eating and laughing and carrying on. And it was, I think, some of his happiest times. Well, at least some of his happiest times at church. I believe it was because it reminded him of happy times on the farm.

LEO AND PRESENTS

One Christmas, George and Lucille were over at our house with some other friends. I was in the kitchen fixing snacks, and the rest of the group was in the living room by the Christmas tree. Leo came out to the kitchen and handed me a brown paper sack.

Leo said, "Merry Christmas!"

"Leo," I said, "Thanks, but I don't like to open my presents before Christmas." I really don't. In fact, I sometimes wait until well after Christmas to open my presents because if I open them, that means that Christmas is over. So, I really do not like to open them before Christmas.

Leo and our grandson Nicholas

"No, I want you to open it now. This is your Christmas present." He was so insistent.

"Oh," I thought, "it must be something really special if he wants me to open it now in front of our friends." Besides, it's too big to be a glass eye, so I was really getting excited!

So, I opened it up. It was a mixer, a hand mixer.

I said, "Oh…this is nice." I was trying so hard not to laugh because he was obviously excited about his gift.

"Yeah," he said. "I want to make eggnog tonight for our guests, so

I thought this mixer would be nice."

"So, my Christmas present is to use tonight?" I asked.

"Yeah, because I want to make them eggnog, and the big blender doesn't do it right. This is your Christmas present!" He was still very pleased with himself.

He then took it out of my hands, mixed up the eggnog, and served it happily to our guests. I just stood in the kitchen and smiled to myself!

LEO AND BLENDERS

Leo always had a thing for blenders, and, really, all small appliances. But blenders were especially his favorite.

He had heard somebody on TV talk about how carrot juice is good for your body, how it keeps up your strength and longevity, and all those good things. So, he bought this very, very, very expensive blender. Every morning and evening, he would have a glass of carrot juice.

His big blenders were only for carrots. Leo insisted that they only be used for carrots. They were big, commercial-grade blenders, capable of doing so much more. Occasionally, he would put in a little apple in with the carrots, but that was it.

Like white cars, he insisted that everybody in his office buy one of these blenders. I really felt sorry for them because they were high-end and very expensive. The people in the office did buy them, and some of them even brought their blenders to work. They would have them in the office and make carrot juice for lunch.

I bet the secretaries and others wished they were working in the plant, so they would not have to buy blenders and white cars. But they were in the office, and those were the rules.

Whenever Leo saw lots of white cars and blenders, it made him happy.

FARM FOOD

Leo did not like to do much of anything besides work and eat, and not necessarily in that order. Leo was an equal opportunity eater. He would eat just about anything you put in front of him, especially if it was seafood.

Leo and my Mom and Dad

The only disagreement we had about food was regarding fish. I do not like to eat fish or even the smell of fish. On the other hand, Leo just loved fish—and the fishier the better! On cruise ships, every night except for prime rib, Leo ate tons of fish because he never got it at home. When we would go out to a meal, he would often order seafood, and he would kid me and say, "I'm going to sit next to you and eat fish!" I would just shrug my shoulder and say, "I'm used to it." I pretended that it did not bother me, but it did.

Where we agreed was farm food. If you have ever tasted farm food, it is so good. Leo came from a farm family, so he was used to having lots of potatoes, gravy, and meats of all kinds. He also liked stews, heavy soups, and anything with hamburger meat. Anything that would typically be on a farm menu. Honestly, he would eat just about anything that was put down in front of him.

Leo especially loved my mother's cooking. I thought my cooking was just like Mom's since I learned from her. Our mothers always have the best way of making things, and Leo could certainly taste a difference. Mom learned to cook farm food from my grandmother, who was the oldest of seventeen children. When my grandmother was in the third grade, her mother took her out of school, put her on a kitchen stool so she could reach the stove, and said, "You will now cook for the family, and all of the farm workers." My grandmother was a fabulous cook, and my mother learned all her recipes, especially how to make the tastiest gravy.

Leo would always ask me, "When are we going over to your mom's house for dinner?" If Mom came by, he would ask, "What are you having for dinner tonight?" He just loved to eat her cooking!

When we were on a cruise, we were nearly always the first ones in the dining room. Our seats were always at the same table, so he could quickly know where to sit down. Leo wanted to be sure to get his order in first. We were always first in the buffet line, too!

I have never been a big eater. I am still not one today. After we were married a while, I said, "Leo this has got to stop. I cannot eat this much!" He was *always* hungry. His favorite meal I made was a vegetable stew. I would make it quite often, and he would be so happy! Leo could *really* eat. And he enjoyed every minute of it. As far as drinking, Leo only ever drank water or carrot juice—that's it.

At home, I pretty much knew the size of his appetite, so I would fill his plate with so many spoonfuls of soup, stew, mashed potatoes, and gravy, or any of those wonderful things. Leo was the type of person that would eat everything on his plate. I barely had to wash the dishes—they were so clean. Of course, I did, but they already looked pretty clean.

When we went out to eat, we would eat quickly, and then go home so he could start designing again. That is why I did not eat much, I could never finish an entire meal! Lots of times I would want to talk, and he would just say *"Shhhh, Shhhhh. We gotta eat fast 'cause I have to get home and finish this drawing."*

"But, Leo," I said, "I haven't even finished my first course." Keeping Leo well-fed was the key to keeping him happy!

SUET PUDDING

Suet pudding is a traditional holiday dish that Dad's mother made. Grandma Dalton was a farm girl. It was kind of a plum pudding, which includes suet, which is lard, along with raisins, and lots of flour. Our family used a big, special steamer to make it, and we steamed it in a flour sack towel.

Mom decided it was her mission that everybody who sat at our table had a bowl of suet pudding, even if they did not want a bowl of suet pudding. So, when Leo joined the family and we had our first holiday together, we had suet pudding.

It was a family tradition, and an initiation to eat at our family table. Most the time, the new person did not like it, and often without taking a bite. Let's face it, it was pudding made out of lard.

I liked it when it was first out of the steamer. It was so good. It was also a family tradition for my mom to present the pudding to my father on a large platter, and he got the first bowl. It was a big, big pudding, around the size of a slightly deflated basketball. Dad would start by slicing a piece off, putting on a little sugar on, and grabbing some milk. Other times, our son, Paul, would make a nice rum sauce on it. To some people, suet pudding tasted like a bar of soap, and it certainly had the same texture.

Dad would ask, "Any more pudding? Any more pudding?" Mom would get out a bowl, put in a hunk, and set out a carton of milk. He would sit there with the parrot on his shoulder and eat this million-calorie pudding. Even at the age of 97, the doctors said he had the arteries of a teenager.

When it was Leo's turn to try it, my mom said, "Leo, bring your bowl over here. You're our virgin for the night. Everybody else at this table already knows that if they want food, they must start off with suet pudding." As opposed to everyone else who ever tried it, Leo just jumped right in without a moment's hesitation. Leo loved it and he ended up eating three bowls. He asked for it all the time. He fit right into our family!

Leo the birthday boy!

LEO'S TREADMILL

Leo had a treadmill in his office at G&L. However, I have never seen it without about two inches of dust on it. I do not think he ever used it, but it looked good. I think he just found it interesting, and, since it was mechanical, he liked having it around.

Even now, when we show someone Leo's office, people always seem impressed that he had a treadmill in his office. They ask, "Oh, did Leo exercise on this?" We all just look at each other, and go, "Uhh, no." He bought it and it looked good, but none of us ever saw him on it. He would not let us get rid of it either, so it just stayed in his office. If anyone ever cleaned the dust off, I do not think I would recognize it. The image with dust has become embedded in my mind.

When he came home, instead of taking a walk around the block or doing another form of exercise, he went into his office to design guitars.

DANCING

Dancing would be considered exercise, so that was not for Leo. On the dance floor, you would never know that Leo was world-famous for revolutionizing music because he had no rhythm. Although he never did dance with me!

When we were on cruise ships, I would say, "Come on, dance with me!" Leo always said, "I can't dance because I can't hear the music. Besides, I don't know how to dance."

My mom and Leo were both born in August, so they both had Leo horoscopes. You had better watch out when two Leos clash! My Leo was a stubborn Leo, but had not met another Leo quite like my mother. She took a more direct approach than I did.

Mom stood up and demanded, "Leo, get up here. Dance with me!"

"No, I don't know how to dance, Hazel."

"Get up here!" she said. "Can't you feel that music in your feet?"

"Yeah." Leo had to admit he could.

"Then you can dance. And you are going to dance with me!" She insisted.

Mom loved to dance, and growing up we were always dancing. Leo complied. She got him up there, and they danced one whole song. Then he said, "Okay, now I don't have to dance anymore."

He looked like he was doing a decent job. He was not stepping on her toes or anything. He could indeed feel the music through his feet, even though his hearing was not good. However, it was not going to be a new career for him. Mom came back to our seats, just laughing hysterically. She told him, "See, Leo? I knew you could do it!".

LEO'S ENERGY

Leo's fried bacon and carrot juice regimen seemed to really work because he generally had a lot of energy.

Leo walked a mile a minute. I have really short legs, and I was always sort of running behind him. He would just take off. Dad was also a fast walker, so Mom and I were used to being left behind! He was a fast walker, and he never seemed to tire. When food was involved, he moved even quicker. However, if he had an idea for an instrument, he would fly!

His energy kept him working about seven days a week unless we were travelling. Even then, he would be working on the ship, while I played the whole time. But for him, work was his playtime. Whenever he could put a new twist to a design, change a sound, or a modify a look, he got energized. For him, a full day working was the best play-day ever.

The rest of the time he just slept, ate, or meditated in his morning bath. I do not mean like a holy man, but like a man that was deep in thought. He would often tell me, "Last night I was thinking about what it would look like if I did this little thing to the guitar." Or, "I wonder how this *little* movement of the strings give a different sound?" That is how his mind worked.

Moving fast or slow, Leo's mind was always on!

CHAPTER 7

A Simple Life

SMALL AND SIMPLE THINGS

Leo liked to keep things simple. For example, when Leo and I went out, Leo liked places like Marie Callendar's, Polly's Pies, or other unassuming places. Occasionally, we went out with other people to a hotel that had a nice dining room. But most the time we liked to keep our casual clothes on.

Leo avoided any kind of fuss. For special occasions, such as our anniversary or birthdays, we went to Sizzler on Harbor Boulevard, and got steaks and baked potatoes. Leo did not really like to dress up. We saved that for our cruises. A couple of times we got a little crazy and went to the Summit House, a nice restaurant on top of Fullerton's highest hill. Leo liked the prime rib there. There were a lot of simple farm roots. He was a farm boy, Mom grew up in South Dakota on a farm, and Dad came from Kansas.

Leo never bragged. If he were ever inclined to brag, it probably would be about white cars, blenders, or musical instruments—never about himself. He was a quiet giant. His life had always been simple, so that made our life together comfortable for both of us. The kids learned all the important things from my family. My sons learned how to treat a woman nicely and how to be polite. My mother taught them how to cook and do laundry. We all went to church. Some people might say this sounds boring, but to me it was beautiful. There was so much love and caring, and Leo sensed it in all we did as a family.

When Leo and I first met, it was clear that he really loved his work. This was simple and direct, and I never wanted Leo to change that. However, I did want to expand his world a little bit, and I invited him into my world with lots of family, potlucks, and laughs. He dived in head first, and really embraced his new life with kids and grandkids. It all worked because my family appreciated the simpler things in life.

Leo expanded my world, too. He introduced me to his world of guitars and music, and what a wonderful world it is! I loved the wonderful people at the plant and the countless people at the conventions and events, not to mention the beautiful guitars themselves. I also love all the musicians, so Leo and I had that in common. Guitars are truly works of art.

I got the guitar world, which I love, and he got a large, fun family, which he loved. It really worked out well for both of us!

LOVE OF FULLERTON

Leo really loved the city of Fullerton. He loved the feel of the town. He was born here, went to school here, started his business here, worked his last day here, and died here. Even when Leo gained fame and fortune, he never considered leaving Fullerton. It was perfect for him. It was not too big, and not too small. It has great weather and is close to the beach, but not too close. It has good housing, but it also has an industrial section of town just perfect to build guitar plants. Fullerton really is wonderful!

There were times when Leo did long for the good old days, when Fullerton was full of orange groves and farms. Yet, even as Fullerton was developed over the years, and the orange groves disappeared, he was still happy and content here.

It was sad for Leo when so many of the orange groves were being taken out, only to be replaced with industrial buildings. He reminisced how it was when he was six or seven years old, with the big farms and the orchards. It smelled so good when the orange blossoms were blooming. There were no freeways. He was kind of sad about the progress…except for the development of his plants!

Occasionally, when we were driving around, he would say, "I used to play in an orange grove right there." Or, "We got vegetables and fruit out of that garden, took them on our truck for the farmer, and sold them all over Anaheim Hills." He would say, "It was always so pretty here in Fullerton."

Even as Fullerton was being developed, Leo was not the kind of person who had to go somewhere else to be happy. He did enjoy an annual cruise, or a weekend trip on his boat to Catalina. However, he was always happy coming home to Fullerton. It had a Carl's Jr., a Sizzler, Polly's Pie, a Spire's restaurant, and his guitar plants. What else could he need?

FOUNDER'S DAY PARADE

For many years, in the summer, Fullerton had a Founders' Day Parade. It was usually dedicated to someone who lived or worked in Fullerton. One year, the theme was music. Who better than Leo to be the Grand Marshal?

He was a little shy, and he wasn't sure he wanted to do it. Again, that's Mr. Quiet. But they had this wonderful old car, and they let me ride along with him. The streets were all filled with people waving and screaming.

I was waving for both of us and he kept saying, "When is this going to be over? I've got to get back to work!"

"No, you don't, no you don't," I said. "This is special."

Leo blurted, "But I really have to get back to work. When's this going to be over?"

"Leo, just have fun!" I said. "Wave at the people."

"I don't know 'em." He responded.

"Just wave anyway!" I insisted.

So he would put his hand up a little, and the people would cheer. Then he asked again, "How long is this parade?" He was not even moved by all the cheering people.

It was a quick parade route down Harbor Boulevard, less than a mile long. It was not like it went on forever. I kept wondering what he was thinking. I should have known what he was thinking. He had a new idea for a pickup or something along those lines. For the entire parade, he kept asking, "How long is this parade gonna be? When's it gonna stop? Do I have to talk? When's it going to be over? I've gotta get back to work." It was as if he had a boss that was expecting him to get back to work.

Leo was Fullerton's Grand Marshall at the Founder's Parade

People were calling out to him, "Hi, Leo! I've got one of your guitars!" Some people had their guitars, and were holding them up for him to see. We rode along, and when we finished he quickly had somebody from the plant come and pick him up. He called on the phone and said, "Come and get me!"

It was not that he did not appreciate that they were honoring him. It was just that Leo did not do anything for the fame or the fortune. He just felt his time was better spent working.

A PURE FOCUS

Leo had a hard time hearing the instruments that he was inventing, but I never heard Leo complain about his hearing loss or the loss of his eye. Not once. Leo's hearing was not the only reason that Leo never learned to play the guitar. Ironically, he felt that having to learn how to play the guitar, or even tuning a guitar, would take his time away from his work designing guitars. He really was *that* driven.

Nothing got in his way. Nothing else mattered. He just had this focus, a singular focus that made him the real deal. He was madly in love with creating his instruments. He would often joke, "I don't have time to play the guitar, I'm too busy making 'em!"

Every major famous musician came by the plant, typically when they were playing a concert at Angel Stadium, the Anaheim Convention Center, or somewhere up in Hollywood. Leo never brought it up, and only told me when I asked. Leo was not star struck in the least, and he did not like it when the stars gushed over him either. To Leo, everyone was just a person.

Leo admired talent. It did not matter one bit if you were famous or not. If you were famous and had no real talent on the guitar, he would just walk away. If you were a kid with talent, Leo would take time to watch. He never asked for an autograph or a picture. If he came out to talk to the stars at all, he just wanted to know about how he could improve their instruments, so he could get back at his drafting table and implement any good suggestions.

At the plant, almost everybody played the guitar. They would sit and talk, and Leo would ask questions. Is the guitar balanced right? Does it need different tuning? Is it comfortable to hold? Is the guitarist satisfied with what they are hearing? My sister, Laurie, plays the guitar, and once she was in Leo's office. He asked her to tune a guitar for him, and then asked her for her opinions about the different features. Leo listened intently to every word she said. He was keenly observant of every musician he saw, even my sweet little sister!

Leo was famous throughout Fullerton for loaning musicians guitars, and then quietly going into the back of the night clubs to watch them play. He would study how the guitarists held the instruments, the balance of it, if the guitars stayed in tune, and he would watch the audience to see how they were enjoying the music.

Leo's world was designing these musical instruments. It was a world that brought him so much joy. I hardly ever saw Leo when he was sad or mad or anything. He was always very level or even tempered, without a lot of ups and downs.

Even if he were at home often, Leo would be on the phone with George or Dale, but he was not one for small talk. His attitude was, "If you want to tell me something, tell me something. Just don't sit and chitchat." That may sound like he was a snob, but he was not. His mindset was just different from many others'. He knew what he had to do. He was way past the point of *wanting* to do something—he *had* to do it. It was his requirement.

WILDA

Leo's sister, Wilda, was a female version of Leo—very quiet. The only time we ever saw her was at Christmas. We would go over to her house in Anaheim and help trim the Christmas tree. We would go and have dinner, and we always brought several big poinsettia plants. We also liked to buy gifts for her two grandchildren.

She wanted so much to please us with dinner; however, she was not the best cook! Everybody would say, "Oh, this is really good, Wilda!" But when she was in the kitchen, we all were shaking our heads, "No, no, no!" I used to go out in the kitchen with her to see if I could help fix anything. She was very charming, and she tried very hard with her cooking.

Every single drawer in her kitchen was stuffed with recipes that she had cut out of magazines and newspapers. One day when I was trying to see if I could help her, I said, "Which of these is your favorite?"

She said, "I've never used any of them."

"Well, why are you keeping them?" I asked.

"Maybe someday I will." She said.

"Well, let's do it next Christmas." I said.

Sadly, we never did. She was so excited to have all those recipes. They were cut out of *everything* you can imagine. She was *so* happy to have the family together. I thought it was sad that Leo did not spend more time with her. She was very innocent, sweet, and family-like, and her two adult boys and their families were delightful.

Leo was just her brother. He was not a big deal to her, just her brother. Her two sons were proud of their uncle, but Wilda was just a good girl, a nice person.

GARAGE SCARE

Leo was used to being the boss, and he brought that attitude home at times. One time, I came home from work, and there were gardeners all around the house, pulling up trees.

"Whoa, whoa, whoa! What're you doing?" I exclaimed.

They said, "Mr. Fender said he wanted them out."

"That was my favorite!" I said pointing to a tree.

Leo did not know how much I liked that tree.

Another time some workers plastered up an entire wall with a sliding glass door. "But those doors looked out onto the pool!" I proclaimed. He forgot to ask me about that, too.

I parked my car in the garage, and Leo would park his outside on the driveway. One day I had to get some groceries, so I got in the car and pushed the button for the garage door to open. I started the car and looked up into the rearview mirror. There was this big man with his arms crossed, and in his hands was a huge machete! I screamed, got out of the car, and ran into the house.

Leo was still home, and I screamed, "Leo there's a man out in the garage!"

He says, "Oh yeah, he's going to do some tree trimming for me."

I pleaded with him, "Will you *please* tell me when there's going to be people around, especially if they're carrying a machete!"

"Well, I thought you were gonna be gone," he calmly replied, unmoved.

I went, "Yeah, now I may have to be going to the hospital! Please, Honey. Please tell me when they're going to be here." It really scared me. When I looked up in that rearview mirror I thought, "Well, this is the end. Lord, here I come!"

Leo just shrugged his shoulders, and said, "Okay." And he went right back to whatever he was working on.

JEWELRY

When Esther and Leo were married, they started off being pretty poor. Leo was starting the business, and then as the business grew he got busy. Leo mentioned that he regretted that he had not bought Esther more jewelry because she loved jewelry.

One year, Leo and I were on a cruise in Venezuela, where they are known for their beautiful emeralds. We took a tour through a jewelry factory, and, of course, we had an opportunity to buy something at the end of the tour.

Leo looked over all the jewelry, spotted a huge emerald ring and said, "We should get you something."

I said, "No, Leo, I really don't wear big stuff. I like little rings. I have fairly small hands and so it's—"

"Yeah," he said. "but it's—it's kind of not too expensive here." And then he got really quiet, and Leo said, "Esther always liked jewelry. And I didn't buy her any." And then he would be silent again. "I should have done that. I should have." He would repeat that over and over. "I should have bought her something. I'm going to buy you something."

"But I don't *need* jewelry," I said. "I have very small hands. I don't need a great big—"

"Let's just go look at them," he insisted, cutting me off.

He saw an emerald ring in one of the cases. It was probably thirty carats or more, it was a *huge* ring! He said, "Well that one is really pretty. You gotta get that one." Pointing to the huge ring.

I said, "Leo, my hand couldn't even *hold* that one." I have little fingers. "Leo, I can't wear that ring."

He said, "But it's so pretty!"

"I *know* it's pretty, Honey, but if you want to buy me something, buy me something little that I will actually wear. Please, find something little."

"You don't like that one?" He asked.

"Yes, I do like it! But I won't wear it! It'll just sit in the drawer. It's too big."

After some pleading, he found a small emerald ring and a little bracelet that had a few little emerald stones. It was simple and it was pretty. It was not as flashy, which suited me fine. We brought them home, and he had such a good time showing them off. He was really happy.

He would say, "I finally did the right thing. I did the right thing."

When I had it on, and people would see them, they would ask where I got it. I would tell them, and Leo would get this great big smile.

It was like he was saying, "I finally did something right."

FAVORITE MUSICIANS

Like anyone, Leo had his favorite musicians.

A lot of people do not realize that Leo's first guitars came out in the 1940s and the Stratocaster came out in 1954. Jimmy Hendrix, the Rolling Stones, and the Beach Boys did not hit the scene until the 1960s and were not the first to the game. Many are surprised to find out that Fender guitars actually took root for years in country music, not rock and roll.

Leo liked farm boy music. He liked country music. He understood country music. He was happy to work with country music, so it could have that *twangy-twang* sound. Ironically, Leo did not understand rock and roll or hard rock music. He appreciated the technical part of it, but often he would turn his hearing aids off for the music itself. Take Elvis, for instance. Of course, Elvis played both a Fender guitar and Fender bass. Leo liked that, but he did not like his hip shaking and strutting.

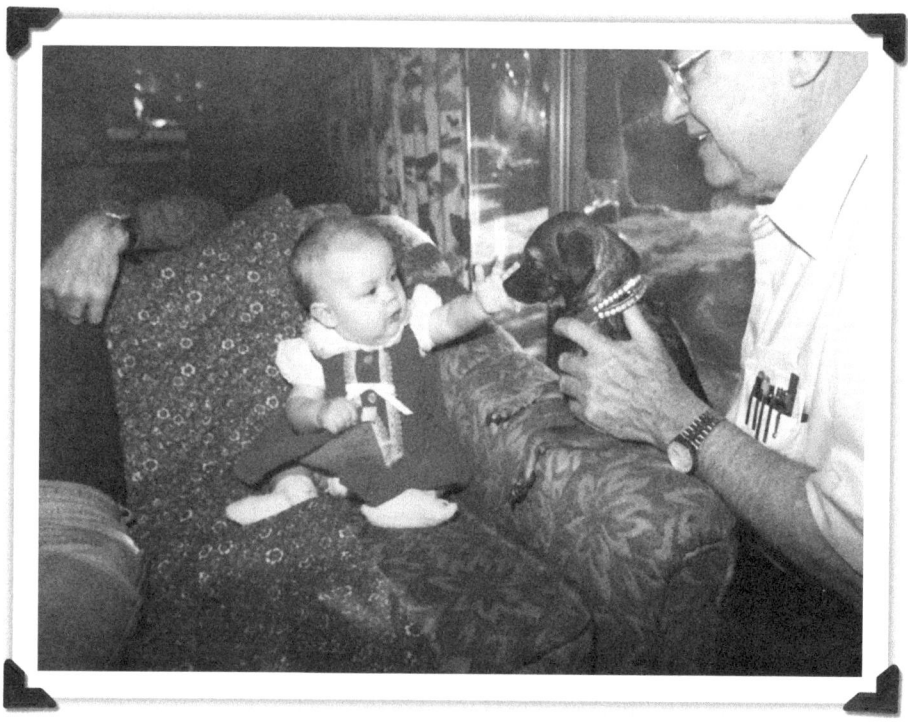

Leo and our first granddaughter Stefani

Leo admired Jimi Hendrix's technical skills, and he thought it was innovative how he used his guitars left-handed. But privately, Leo was not happy about Jimi smashing Stratocasters or setting fire to them. Those guitars were his babies. To Leo, that was like somebody swatting your kids. Those *were* his children and it pained him to see somebody beat it until it was smashed up completely, set fire to it, or just being horrible to it. It was not just Jimi Hendrix, there have been others. But Jimi Hendrix was probably the main one that did horrible things to Leo's guitars. Leo spent all his energy in making a beautiful, high-quality musical instrument, and he always treated the guitars with tender care and respect.

Leo felt that instruments were supposed to bring beautiful music to the world and make us happier. And if we are happier, then the world is going to be a better place. Smashing a guitar on stage or setting it on fire—what does that accomplish? What does that bring? Maybe it gets some *oohs* and *ahhs* from some cuckoos in the audience, but it does not bring beauty to the world.

Leo's favorite musician was Glenn Campbell. Leo felt he was one of the best guitarists. Leo also liked the Sons of the Pioneers and Glen Miller. He was very fond of all of them. At the Country Music Award Shows, all the musicians were turning around talking to Leo and asking him questions about the guitars. All the musicians were always lovely, kind people. His favorite male singer and song were Ray Price singing "For the Good Times." His favorite female singer was Janie Frickie. He also loved Buck Owens. When Barbara Mandrel was about 10 years old, she would come in and Leo would make instruments just for her, and he would make them bigger and bigger as she grew up. He really liked her.

Leo liked country music, but even some of the country music was getting a little rough around the edges for him. He liked *plunkity-plunkily-plunk* music. He was not crazy about jazz. The blues were okay, as long as it did not get too wild. Overall, he liked quiet music.

No matter what music they played, Leo loved musicians. If he didn't like the music itself, he would still be happy that everyone was smiling and having a good time.

LEO'S STUFF

Leo liked having a good car, not a status brand, but one that was mechanically sound. Overall, he shunned the trappings of executive power. Perhaps some would see it as a luxury, but Leo always kept a spare car in the driveway, because he was afraid that if the battery died, it would keep him from getting to work. So instead of keeping a spare battery handy, he kept an extra car handy. In Leo's mind, this was not a luxury, but a necessity, and it seemed practical to him.

Like everything else, Leo's office was custom built for him. Again, Leo bucked tradition, which would dictate that a world-famous millionaire and CEO would have a large office, mahogany panel walls, pictures taken with important people lining the walls, mementoes of success, and, of course, a stellar view of the little people down below.

Leo's office is somewhat hilarious as it has none of that. It is on the ground floor of a nondescript industrial building with no view and has sprayed popcorn ceilings, florescent lights, white drywall, and tile floors.

Guitar Player magazine described Leo's office well, stating:

> *It might disappoint the lowliest federal bureaucrat in Washington. It's a small room, sparsely furnished — no carpet, functional lighting, with a drafting table piled high with blueprints. The monotonic paint is vaguely institutional. A metal bookcase is crammed with speaker parts and catalogs from electronics suppliers. A side door opens into a large room full of industrial drills and punch presses. On the modest desk is a Styrofoam coffee cup that, while disposable, is nevertheless being saved; it is labeled with a name carefully printed on masking tape in ballpoint pen: Leo."*

No one would guess that the occupant of this office was a living legend and an icon. The occupant did not see himself that way.

LEO THE PATRIOT

Leo said many times that, other than his name on the instrument, the stamp *Made in the USA* was the most beautiful thing about his guitars. He was a proud American, and he wanted everything made in the USA!

Leo was so patriotic. When we would go to parades and the flags went by, he would get a tear in his eye as he held his hand on his heart. He was not much into sports, so he did not watch the Olympics or anything like that, but whenever there was a moment when we were all proud to be Americans, he was the proudest about his country. He loved the United States of America.

Leo always went outside, and hoisted the flag up for the holidays. As he did that we would both have tears, and he would put his hand over his heart. He said many times how much he loved the United States.

Leo always voted Republican. Leo really liked Ronald Reagan and the only thing hanging in his office when he died was a picture of President George H. W. Bush and First Lady Mrs. Bush. He did not even have a picture of me anywhere in his office. He was a true conservative. He was less interested in conservative laws, but more interested in conservative concerns. He was less interested in the debate between Republicans and Democrats. He wanted everyone to be *concerned* with what was going on in the United States. Whether that took a Republican or a Democrat, Leo was for whoever was bringing the United States to the best place that it could be.

Leo would be disappointed at the state of the country right now. He would not like the lack of pride in our country that some Americans have or the outsourcing of manufacturing and jobs to foreign countries. He would not be happy with a war just to get someone else's oil. Leo believed whatever we were doing as a country should be for the betterment of both us and others.

Leo in the Caribeean

CHAIN-LINK FENCES & GARBAGE CANS

It was interesting just how much Leo and I saw the world so differently. We would go on these beautiful cruises to wonderful places all around the world. After we were married, Leo bought a camera for me. It had so many lenses and different parts, and all these lenses and parts intimidated me. I fumbled around and took the camera along on a couple of cruises. But I could never take a decent picture, so one day I finally said, "Leo, I can't manage this camera. By the time, I figure out how to fix the lens and do all that, whatever I wanted to take a picture of is gone."

He looked at me with an odd expression on his face, because he loved that camera so much. Yet he took the camera back, and bought me a little point-and-shoot camera.

We were always taking pictures when we traveled. When we would get home, I would take my film down to my local drug store, and he would take his film to a professional place. Mine would come back quickly, and there would be beautiful sunsets, children playing on the beach, flower arrangements, waves, and the ship.

Leo's professional pictures would come back after a while, and there would be motors, chains, and all kinds of equipment. On cruises, he would get permission to go down in the engine room of the ship and take pictures of all the equipment down in the dirty, hot engine room. We would walk around town, and there would be all this beauty, but Leo would be taking a picture of a chain-link fence.

At home, when he would get a new camera, he would take rolls and rolls of film of our garbage cans! He would do it from every angle, and with every setting on the camera to test out his new toy. From the pictures we took, it never looked like we were on the same cruise or even on the same planet!

I would laugh, but he did not find it funny at all. I would ask him where the pictures were of all the beautiful things we had seen. "Well," he would say. "I knew you were taking those pictures, so I didn't have to." But he never really looked at mine. He would glance at them, but I _knew_ that he liked his photos better.

CHURCH SOUND SYSTEM

Even though Leo went to church as a child, it was not until after we had been married for a while that Leo would come to church somewhat regularly. Otherwise, the only time Leo really came to church was when I sang in the choir for some special event, such as for a Christmas or Easter musical. I would insist that he come with me to hear us, which he did. However, I noticed from the choir loft that he would always be sitting very close to the front, and he would not be paying attention to the choir music. He was sort of looking around.

Afterwards he would say, "You know what, your sound system would be a lot better if you installed this, this, this or that." Or, "Those tiles you've got in your ceiling sure are absorbing the sound. You ought to change them out." He would also look over the lighting, and he would tell me what kind of lighting system we should get instead.

The whole time we were trying to sing our beautiful music, and I would see him just looking around and studying the acoustic design. He would get out his little notebook out of his pocket, and take notes of all the modifications we should make, but the church never did!

COUNTRY AWARDS SPEECH

Leo loved the Country Music Association awards ceremony. He really enjoyed watching them on television. He loved country music. It was his very favorite. One year, the event was hosted at the auditorium in Knott's Berry Farm, just south of Fullerton in Buena Park. They had secretly contacted me to tell me that Leo was going to win the Founder's Music Award, but it was to be a secret! I was so excited and nervous at the same time.

Leo would be uncomfortable speaking to two or three people, much less several million people on TV. I tried to think of a way to prepare him or make it less uncomfortable for him.

One night I said, "Oh, are we going to go to the awards?"

"Yeah, we'll go," he said. "We'll go."

"What would you say if they gave an award to you?" I pretended not to know the truth.

"Well, that's not going to happen." He responded quickly.

"Let's just pretend," I said. "What would you say if they handed you the award?"

"It's not going to happen, so why are we even talking about it?" He continued to insist.

"We're just *pretending,* Honey. We're just pretending."

I did not want him to stand up there and stammer, mumble, or say nothing, which would be even worse. So, I kept after him, but he would not play along.

The day of the show I was so nervous. I was perspiring, and I do not normally perspire. I was just so nervous for him I could hardly stand it. When they finally called his name, he got up and looked back at me—and not with a pleasant look.

"Yeah, I knew you'd get it," I said. As he walked up to the podium I started praying, *"Please, Lord. Please, Lord. Please, Lord."* I prayed that he would not embarrass himself. Remember, Leo was a *silent* giant after all, with an emphasis on the silent part.

He walked up to the microphone, leaned in, and then said, "Music has been very good to me, thank you." That was it! He said it in this lovely, sincere voice, and he meant what he said. With that Leo walked away to a grand, standing ovation. It was perfect, and I was so relieved.

CHAPTER 8

Inside Leo's Head

CANDY APPLE RED

I n the days before Leo Fender, all guitars were basically brown, acoustic boxes. Acoustic guitars are beautiful, and they produce beautiful music, but guitars had been sort of stuck in this mode forever.

Then my Leo showed up. The first time the two words "Leo" and "flamboyant" have shown up in the same sentence, is this one. He was a simple farm boy. Yet, inside the mind of this simple man was an explosive, creative energy like the world had never seen.

First, when Leo electrified the guitar, he broke the sound barrier. Overnight, the guitar went from a limited sound, to hundreds, thousands, or really infinite sounds. While the electric guitar could mimic the acoustic sounds, with the switch of a button it would explode into a rainbow of sounds. Because of Leo's invention, *Webster Dictionary* had to add a lot of new words, like hard rock, classic rock, surfer music, grunge, new wave, and on and on. Not many people have that on their list of accomplishments.

Leo knew he was creating a sound that had never been heard

before. Honestly, he did not always like the sounds that his guitars were making, but he knew he was helping these angel musicians do what they were called to do. That would have been enough for most people, but it was not enough for Leo.

Leo must have asked himself, "Why not take these new guitars, and all the infinite sounds they produced, and paint them candy-apple red? In fact, why not take them and paint them blue, pink, yellow, purple, green, orange, and every other imaginable color? Why not add rainbow colors, starbursts, surfer stripes, sparkle paints, and turtle-shell pickguards?" Now they not only sounded different, but they looked incredible.

I would joke with Leo that all his guitars screamed, "Look at me!" This was rather ironic because those of us who knew him, knew Leo would never want this attention for himself. It is interesting to wonder how this simple farm boy turned into Mr. Rock and Roll. It's just a wonder of creativity in its highest form.

Leo took another giant leap forward when he challenged traditional thinking yet again. He did this by asking "Why not take these new electric guitars that sound incredible and look amazing, and take them in new places? Why not take music from its comfortable roots in concert halls and stages, and take them outside into the open and to every possible location?" Now the rest of the world had something new to really think about.

Leo may have looked mild and unassuming, yet the simplicity of his thinking was truly innovative. Leo's "You won't part with yours either" advertising campaign was the cherry on the top of his incredible music revolution. Leo produced ads featuring guitars with guys and gals at the beach, on surfboards, sailing, dirt biking, camping, sky diving, and even getting a haircut!

When Leo launched this ad campaign, he asked Bob Perline to do it. Bob said, "I went to the beach, hired this guy on the spot—sorry, I don't remember his name—paid him a little money, had him sign a waiver. He slung the Jaguar over his shoulder, paddled out on his board, turned around, and took off on the first good wave. He stood up, whipped the guitar around in front, I snapped the photo, and he finished riding the wave into shore. We got it—one wave, first take. There wasn't a drop of water on that guitar when he came in, either. We packed it back up, and it went back to the factory and got shipped."

Leo told me that, with all the explosions in innovation he was creating, this ad campaign was a bold move, even for him. He was a very confident man, but this even had him a bit nervous. It was all so new, all so surprising, all so controversial, and all so wonderful!

Leo relaxing in Alaska

My Leo turned the music world upside down. He truly electrified everything he touched! With each new invention, Leo added layer upon layer of amazing new possibilities on the musical landscape. For the first time in the history of the world, a guitarist could pick just the sound, look, and image that they wanted. The sound could be soft or loud, and they could add sustain or distortion effects, phasers, wah-wah pedals, and anything else. Finally, every guitar player could fully express their music and what they were all about. This is exactly what Leo wanted guitarists to do.

Leo left the world with a gift so huge, that the music world has yet to find its limits. There are endless possibilities with music that Leo's instruments have the potential to create. Because of the electric guitar and electric bass, today's musicians can fill up entire arenas, entertain the crowd for hours, and create lifetime memories. Music will spend hundreds of years exploring, creating, entertaining, and expanding on the vision that Leo created.

It has always amused me that, inside the mind of this ordinary looking farm boy, was one of the most explosive, creative energies that the world had ever seen. When it comes to today's music, in one way or another, all roads lead to Leo.

A SHY GUY

Leo was at the apex of the music world. Fans would chase musicians for their autographs, but the musicians would chase Leo! Often when we were on a cruise ship, we would open the cabin door, and there would be two or three musicians outside like groupies wanting a picture. He thought that was amusing, but Leo never really understood his importance in the world.

Leo was very shy. Some people thought he came across as being stuck up. However, if one was around him for a longer time, they would understand that was just him. Often, when we were in public, he would push me ahead of him to talk to people first. Then, if I could figure out something about the person that Leo could relate to, I would tell him what it was, and step aside. Yet even with a prompt from me, he would not have long conversations with anyone, even with people he knew for years.

Many people like admiration or enjoy being complimented, but not Leo. Most of the people we met were so lovely, and they wanted to praise him, but Leo did not want to hear it. If you liked Leo or didn't, it did not matter to him; however, he did care about what people were saying about his inventions.

Fullerton High School inducted Leo onto their Wall of Fame as an honored alumnus. They invited us to a spaghetti dinner in the gymnasium before a football game. We brought along a few friends. During the ceremony, they asked Leo to come up and say a few words. He was so shocked, he just turned white.

He quickly grabbed my hand and said, "Come on!" He pulled me up on the stage, and stood behind me. He just stood there and said, "You talk."

I said, "They don't want me here. What do I have to say?" So, I just cheered on the football team and thanked them for the honor. As we started to go down, he leaned over to the microphone and quickly said, "Thank you."

He only wanted to talk about important things, like guitars. While he was painfully shy in public, he had no problem talking at the plant. There, he plainly spoke his mind. He did not dislike people, but he did not have social graces where one, just out of common courtesy, interacts with others.

Leo's isolation thing did not only apply to strangers, it even applied to me! Once on a trip to Germany, Leo had packed his own suitcase. I reminded him several times about what he needed to bring. I was talking to him on the plane, but he was not paying any attention to me. Finally, I kind of punched at him.

"Leo, did you bring batteries for your hearing aid?"

"What?" He asked.

I said, "Did you bring batteries for your hearing—"

"What?" he asked again, a little louder this time.

I noticed that he did not even have his hearing aids in. I said loudly, "Did you bring your hearing aids?"

"Yes."

I said, "Then why don't you put them in, so I can talk to you?"

"Well, I'm saving the batteries until something important comes along."

I sat there, smiling. He often said things like that, but he was not being mean. I never took offense to his comments. Leo was who he was—there was no sense getting upset. That is how he felt about life. He was very practical. He saved his batteries, and I just grinned and read my book all the way to Germany.

GIRLS IN TIGHT JEANS

Leo appreciated beauty. Specifically, if there was a pretty girl in tight jeans anywhere within view, Leo's eyes immediately went there. I teased Leo about it, and it was one of the few things I could tease him about. I knew he would never take it any further, he just appreciated beauty. The guys at the plant would tease him about it too. He simply could not control himself!

"Leo," I said, when I noticed him eyeing a pretty girl, "that's not nice."

"Yes, it is," he'd say.

If we would walk behind a pretty lady and he would stand there and look and look and look until they got so far away, you could not see them anymore. "You're a nasty old man!" I would tease him.

"Yes, I am." He said, "They just look so nice."

If a pretty girl in tight jeans was walking in front of us, he would often say, "My, my, my." I just laughed, he was lucky I was not the jealous type.

LEO'S SENSE OF HUMOR

For a quiet man, Leo loved to laugh loudly. He would laugh and he had a *big* laugh. For this quiet giant of a man, he could laugh like crazy. You could hear him across the plant. Laugh and hug—he could even do both at the same time.

Leo enjoyed teasing others, but he was not as excited when he was the one being teased! He was an interesting guy who had more than his fair share of idiosyncrasies, but he did not like to be teased about them, and you certainly could not tease him about his guitars. He never really understood the double-standard in this behavior!

On the other hand, he thought it was great fun when he could say some silly thing about what someone else was doing. Leo also thought it was fun to play tricks on people. Leo never played tricks on me, but mostly he would do it to the guys at the plant.

Leo's offbeat humor kept the employees entertained. When I visited the plant, often the workers would share his joke of the day. Leo was fond of saying that everyone thinks all of our guitars are "'custom,' because all of our competition 'cussed 'em!'" Leo also had a bunch of little sayings. For example, if he was talking about paying attention to priorities, he would say, "Well, we can't keep everything in the top sock drawer!"

Leo's work clothes sometimes created a false impression that he was a man of limited means, and oftentimes he was mistaken as one of the plant workers. If a stranger wandered into the plant and was unkind to anyone, Leo would quietly take him apart with his sharp wit and sarcasm.

One of Leo's favorite pastimes was to annoy know-it-all salesmen regarding something about their own products, and then he would go on to explain details of the product that the salesperson did not know. Soon the former know-it-all figured out just who they were speaking to.

Guitar Player magazine tells of a time when Leo, George and Forrest White went into a Cadillac dealership. The salesman looked them over. He was not very nice. Not knowing who Leo was, the dealer, Forrest recalls,

> . . . *took one look and figured, 'Heck, these guys couldn't buy a Cadillac between the three of them! And he very definitely let us know that he wasn't interested in wasting time on us." Leo was miffed, and he questioned whether the car's seat was genuine leather. The indignant salesman assured the "workman" that they certainly were. Leo disagreed and started a heated, extended argument, claiming that the seat covers were made of oilcloth. When the salesman reached the boiling point, Leo cracked, "Well, it really doesn't matter – I only need it for a work car anyhow!*

One of the most priceless stories happened in the Fender plant on Raymond Avenue. By this time, the company had hired hundreds of people. True to his nature, Leo would emerge from his lab daily and stroll along the production line. When Leo came across a new employee, he made a few suggestions about how the guy could do his work better. The new guy popped off, "Hey buddy! I'll do my job, and you do your job! Ok?!" Leo did not let him know who he was or get angry, he just said, "Ok," grinned, and walked off.

Everyone in the plant heard this exchange and just laughed and laughed! Of course, this new guy never lived it down and was teased about it for the rest of his days. While everyone got a good laugh, it provides great insight into the kind of man Leo was. He was in total control of his emotions. Leo not only had a high IQ intellectually, but also a high IQ emotionally.

Many times a visitor would come to the plant and get a little tour. They would then point to a man sitting quietly off in the corner working with a screwdriver, and ask, "Who's that?" The answer was always, "This is his joint. He owns everything."

LEO AND BOATS

Leo lived very simply. He lived well below his means, but he did love boats. He especially loved the mechanics of them. Over his life, Leo owned four beautiful, sixty-foot-long cabin cruisers. His routine for purchasing a boat was predictable. Leo called a boat manufacturer in the Bay Area and told them he was interested in purchasing a boat. However, he wanted to have a say in its design, how it looked, and all the exact features he wanted.

The manufacturers would send over the blueprints, and then Leo would go to his drafting table to modify them. Leo would send them back, and then Leo and the manufacturer would go through a long dance of back and forth, and back and forth. Leo's modified boats were beautiful. True to his nature, his boats were not fancy, but they were certainly seaworthy with no frills. They were beautifully designed and fully functional.

Leo loved to design anything, and he was good at it. Leo should have gotten design royalties, because the manufacturers would keep Leo's ideas and use them in the other boats they made!

Leo had the number one slip at Catalina, right by the casino. He mainly kept his boats at the Long Beach pier, and he always had a crew on call. When Leo wanted to set sail, he would call them, and tell them to get the boat fired up. The crew was there when he came back to clean up the boat.

Captain Leo!

Leo liked to sail over to Catalina just about every weekend. Yet, as everyone around me knows, I go to church on Sunday. I sing in the choir, and I taught Sunday school for many years. I told Leo that I could go every other weekend, but not every weekend.

"Yes—yes, you can," he insisted.

"Leo," I said, "this is really important." I did not mind that he had the boat and if he went to Catalina with friends and family, but I could not go along every single Sunday.

Leo really loved that boat, but one day, out of the blue, he told me that he had sold it. I never asked him to, but that was just how Leo did things. Six or seven years later, one of his boats became available, along with the prime slip in Catalina. Leo was interested and said, "You know, we should go out and see it." However, by this time his Parkinson's Disease had started, and I was very concerned for his safety. Leo always captained his own boats, and never let anyone else do it. He would power it over there and back, and he just loved being at sea, so I knew it would be impossible to fully enjoy his boat if he was not the captain.

He still wanted to go and check it, because he thought that our kids would really enjoy it. But our kids were going in ninety different directions. They were starting new families, and they were doing everything with their own families. They would have enjoyed a boat some of the time, but not every weekend as Leo wanted. I felt sad because he loved boats so much, but with Parkinson's taking over his body, his sailing days were over and we both knew it.

GAY PRIDE PARADE

One of my funniest memories with Leo was one that he never found out about.

Leo and I had gone to an event in Chicago with some other people from the company. It was a music show with a lot of musicians and instruments. They were really kind to us, and they put us up in a nice hotel and provided us with a driver. We were there for three or four days.

The organizers took us to where the Chicago Cubs played baseball, and we got to walk out on the field. They took us up to the top floors of some of those tall buildings that scare you to death because it feels like you are going to fall right out the window. We were just having a really good time, being treated like royalty.

After some time enjoying the view from one of the skyscrapers, the driver said, "I need to get you guys back in time for the get-together at the show." So, down the elevator we went, and we got into a limousine. The driver pulled out of the parking garage onto a very large street.

I looked out the car window and I remarked, "Boy, there are a lot of people here!" There were huge crowds lining both sides of the street!

Leo looked out the window, and said, "I didn't know that they knew I was here. Did you guys tell them that I was here?" Now, Leo was not a proud man, but we had been treated so well, and the comment just sort of came out of his mouth.

"Look Leo," I said, "they are all waving." He rolled down the window and Leo was waving out the window. People were clapping and cheering. The crowd was going wild!

I really did not know what was going on. We had not had crowds like that following us the rest of our visit. I finally turned around and looked out the rear window and saw a whole parade of people coming down the street. They were carrying a huge sign that said, "Gay Pride Day in Chicago." I thought to myself, "Oh, wow!" I just grinned to myself.

Leo had been a parade grand marshal before, and he thought that this was a surprise parade for him! He was having so much fun! That was unusual for him, but seeing the reaction from the crowd one could not help but have fun. Leo was smiling, waving out the window, and the crowd was going crazy, and yelling and saying "Yay! Yay!"

The driver started laughing so hard, we almost crashed! He drove us on the parade route for blocks and blocks waving to thousands of people, with a band playing behind us. At the end of the parade, Leo said, "That was really nice!"

I have to confess that I never told Leo what was really going on. That will be our little secret!

CHRISTMAS TUNA

One Christmas, Leo and I were over at George and Lucille's. We had just walked in the door, and Leo said, "Just a minute," and ran back to the car. He came back with a brown paper sack. Handing it to me, he said, "I brought you a Christmas present! I want you to have this!"

I opened it up, and inside that brown paper bag was an umbrella and twelve cans of tuna. Really! That was it.

Leo on a helicopter tour

Now, I do not eat seafood, and Leo knew that, but every year there was a special cannery down at the beach for those who like seafood. Every year, Leo handed out these bags of special tuna to his friends and family.

Giving cans of tuna for Christmas was not a practical joke. He did not see the humor in it at all, and he thought that was the best present because he loved it so much. Not being a fish eater, I could not say if it was good or bad—it all smells rotten to me.

Leo would order twenty cases of it and would give it to special people. He gave it as a crown jewel to the people that he liked. Wilda, his sister, always got one. My folks always got one. My folks thought it was fabulous—the best that *they* had ever tasted. And I got one. Oh, goody!

He was very proud of that tuna, and he ate all the ones he gave me. He never thought that it was bizarre that year after year, he would give me the same Christmas present, and then eat it all himself! As a bonus, Leo kept all the empty, washed cans to keep nuts and bolts in at his workbench.

Leo saved all the cans he found. In fact, he loved empty cans. He had one customer from Germany, and every Christmas they sent this *huge* tin box of cookies. They were very good, and the tin was beautiful. We kept a lot of those for a long time until my mother stole a few of them. Other people said, "You've got so many can we just have *one*?" So, we shared. Leo ate a lot of nuts, peanuts mostly, and he saved those cans too!

Over the years, Leo gave me many, many, many cases of this tuna. Even though I kept saying, "Honey, I don't eat tuna." He would then just say, "Well, somebody will." It did not matter to him if I ate them or not.

A NIGHT AT THE MOVIES

I had a night out at the movies with Leo. Literally, one night.

Leo never went to movies, but I enjoy them. One night, I talked Leo and my parents into going to see the movie *E.T.* I just loved that movie! At some point, I looked over at Leo and noticed that he just had a look on his face that said something like, "What the heck?"

I leaned over to Leo and said, "Just pretend that you're a child and that this is just a show for fun."

After the movie, I ask Leo what he thought, and he said, "I hated it! What was that all about? That has absolutely nothing to do with reality!" I just laughed, and I tried to explain to Leo about wonderful childhood fantasies. Leo was not buying it. Leo's childhood had no room for fantasy; it was just full of chores.

We agreed that next time, I would go to the movies with one of the kids or grandkids, but Leo was done. Leo went to one movie in his whole life, and never went again!

CAL'S CAMERA

Leo loved cameras, not photography, and there is a big difference.

Leo was addicted to cameras, and Cal's Camera was his supplier. Leo had an arrangement with them that, whenever a new camera came in, if it were anything they felt that he might be interested in, they would call and say, "Mr. Fender, we have a new camera in. Would you be interested?" They knew exactly what he liked.

Occasionally, Leo would go down to their store in Costa Mesa, and spend long periods of time looking over all the cameras and discussing all their products. However, most of the time, they would send the cameras to him. The shop would send a delivery man down to the plant with the new camera. For a few weeks or even months, Leo would try out the cameras. He was always interested in all the new cameras coming to market. "How come you don't have to pay for those?" I always asked. "I'm not doing anything; I'm just borrowing them." Everyone at Cal's seemed to be fine with the arrangement.

Leo loved his time at Cal's Camera. He was very proud that they trusted him enough to let him have a camera for months without paying for it. He was *very* excited when he would come home with a new camera. He would play with them in his home office, and go outside to take pictures.

Leo loved camaras, not necessarily photography!

Just like Leo made guitars he never played, he had cameras he never really took any good pictures with. He would take pictures of trash cans around the house. People think I'm joking, but he really did! He loved anything functional or mechanical. Seriously, he would take pictures of our trash cans, and then compare the quality and tone to other pictures he had taken with other cameras of the same trash cans. He walked around and took pictures of our yard. While on a cruise, I would take pictures of the beautiful beaches and sunsets, while Leo would walk around the ship taking pictures of flanges, hinges, and anything mechanical.

If he liked the camera, he sent them a check. Other times he would say, "Well, I think I'll send it back." He would send it back, and they would accept it with no charges. They did this for years and years.

LEO'S AESTHETICS

Leo's aesthetic sense never showed in anything except his guitars. In fact, I can say with complete honesty that 100% of Leo's aesthetic abilities went towards his guitars…not to his clothes, office, or anything else!

He was very much the farm boy. I never knew if he saw the beauty in anything but his work. I know that I sound like a broken record, but Leo's only real joy was work. It is not that he was unhappy—actually, he was quite happy. It was not that he did not like to be around people, and it is not that he was so shy that he *could* not be around people. He just was driven. Some people are driven to paint. There are those who are driven to be a chef. Leo was driven to create these guitars, pianos, electric banjoes, pianos, or all sorts of musical things.

Leo saw a different beauty than most people. To him, electronics were his beauty. But as far as what most people would see as beautiful, like trees waving in the breeze, or the sunset, they were not his beauty. He saw beauty in other things. He saw beauty in design.

Leo's intense concentration on guitars ultimately produced something exceptionally beautiful, even if he did not see them that way. I think that Leo's guitars are works of art, and I have met many people that hang them on their walls instead of paintings!

KEEP NO GUITARS

Most of us, when we are proud of something that we have accomplished, like to keep a memento to enjoy or to show off to friends. It could be a book, painting, or anything else that has your heart. People always ask me, "Which guitar did Leo keep?" *Leo never kept one.* Most look at me in disbelief. They are not sure I am telling the truth. Leo never kept one single guitar.

Leo never brought anything home from the office. He did not ever bring one guitar home! I brought one home because the kids wanted to play with it, but it was kept in a closet most of the time. Leo never kept one guitar. He wanted them all in the hands of musicians!

Leo always said, "The next one I build is going to be so much better. Why would I keep something that was obsolete?" He truly believed that.

While that was probably true, it sure would have been nice to have one of his early ones. Not to sell, but to have for the history of it—to know that his hands had been on that guitar. Both G&L and Fender have given me several beautiful guitars which I love, but they were not made by Leo's own hands. I would have loved to have had one of his.

BRIDGING THE GENERATIONS

To really understand Leo's mindset, one must remember that he did not play the guitar, nor could he even tune a guitar. His entire life's work was for the betterment of other people, but they generally were not his contemporaries. Leo's life work was to reach out to people who were usually much younger than he was.

Leo simply loved every guitar and bass player he met!

At the plant, it was an astonishing sight. On one side, at Fender and G&L, you had quiet, well-groomed, mild-mannered, mechanical engineers, sitting around with loud, long-haired flower-powered hippies and rockers! On the surface, they had absolutely nothing in common, and yet they loved and respected each other!

The whole invention of the electric guitar created an interesting bridge between generations. It would not be unusual for Leo, Freddie, Doc, George, Pete, and others to happily sit for hours with insane rock and roll guitarists. It did not matter if they were wildly famous, or just starting out in music. The passion that both sides of the table had for these instruments is what brought them together, and created an unlikely connection between two generations that were otherwise on two different planets.

When I would visit the plant, it was wonderful to see this connection between a middle aged, mild-mannered mechanical engineer with a plastic pocket protector in their short-sleeved buttoned up dress shirts, engaged in passionate conversations with a wild rocker. Yet, there would be a look of mutual appreciation in their eyes. I am not sure how often this connection happened outside of the Fender or G&L plants, but within those walls, it was an everyday occurrence. It was such great fun. I loved to see all these different people just talking, joking, eating snacks, and just plain enjoying what they were doing together!

It was as if Leo's older generation deliberately reached out to the hippie generation, and used all their skills to connect with them. The younger generation appreciated this and reached back. It was a wonderful world that Leo created, and it worked beautifully!

CHAPTER 9

Business with Leo

LEO THE BOSS

Leo ran the business his way, and it worked beautifully. He was making beautiful instruments, and his employees were happy when I would go to visit them. Often at lunchtime, I would bring them some sort of treats and would sit and talk with them. It was a fun place to be.

His office was fascinating in a Leo kind of way. There was an outer office where his secretary sat. Leo liked his privacy, and his office had two areas to it. When you first walked in, it had his big desk and a drafting table. The second area Leo was fond of calling his "lab." Leo spent most of his time in the lab. There were two military-green tables with electronic testing equipment, soldering irons; custom stands to hold guitars and hundreds of little drawers for electronic components like resisters and capacitors. There were no windows in his lab.

He liked space around him so that he could generate his mental powers. He did not want to be closed in too tightly. He thought very carefully about a new guitar or a new way of doing something. He would do this thinking at the drafting table, then take those drawings into the lab, and create what he had dreamed up on paper. Leo built his designs with his own hands.

In his lab, Leo made guitar prototypes that allowed him to slide the pickups under the strings without actually mounting them. This allowed him to test dozens of pickups quickly with a particular neck. He tried hundreds of pickup designs until he got just the combination he liked. He did this with every single component of the guitar, right down to the smallest screw.

Leo took this picture to test out a new camera

Leo really loved the variety of his designs, from the monochromatic white Tele with a white pick guard and maple neck to Eric Clapton's "black beauty" Strat, and everything in-between. He smiled with the '50s powder blues and the '60s fire engine reds. He studied the various types of wood grains like a mad scientist. They all had to shine with a perfect clear varnish finish, but underneath all the flash, they had to be solid, precise, and functional instruments. Leo was hands-on in every single detail. He wanted the musician to look good, sound good, and feel good.

In his typical process, when Leo got everything perfected, he would take his blueprints and prototypes out to the guys in the plant. Working together, they would get it all set up on the production line. Often, he would need to invent the machine to make it do exactly what he had in mind, or if not invent it, he certainly modified it. Leo's process went from his office's drafting table to the lab, and then from the lab to the plant. All the modern music you hear all over the world originated from Leo's little territory. This whole process happened within a radius of about one-hundred feet.

Leo spent hours and hours designing and testing guitars here

Leo did not sit in an ivory tower. He was not a dreamer; he was a doer. I never saw him read a book, magazine, or newspaper. He might make a rare exception for *Guitar Player* magazine, or some other trade magazine, but that was it.

In 1978, *Guitar Player* magazine asked Leo the question that many had on their minds, "Do you think that perhaps you work too hard?" Leo responded, "Well, it's what I know. Most every evening I'm up until twelve or one o'clock, sketching at home – guitar bodies, pickups, or whatever's necessary."

He would walk all around the plant several times a day. He checked on the production levels, the machinery, and the quality of the workmanship. He knew every square inch of the place. He developed different kinds of drill presses. He would buy machines and then modify them. He did that with many things.

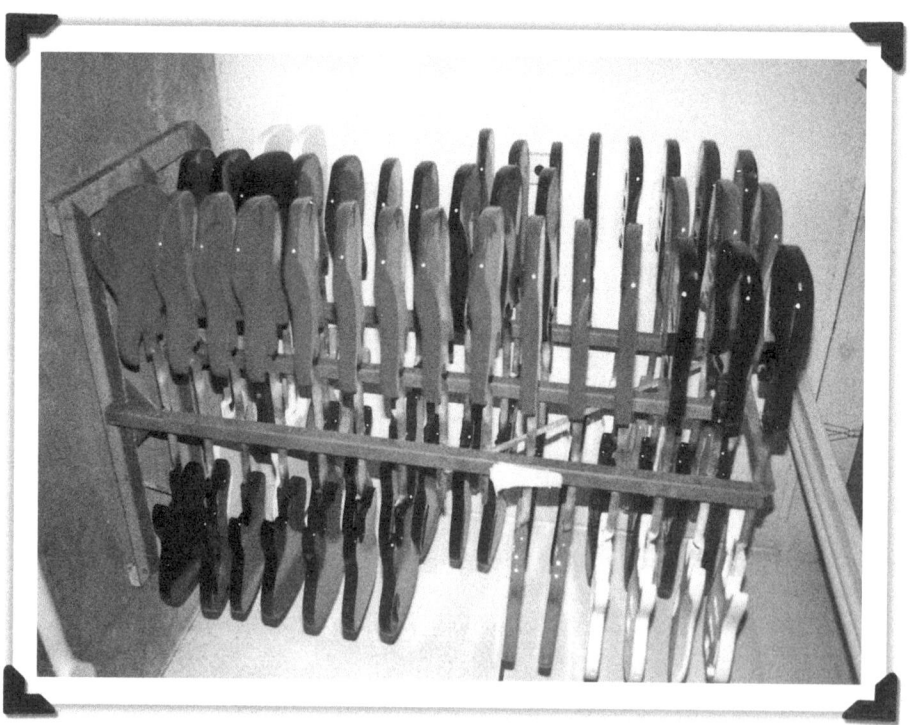

Leo loved to see his guitars coming off the production line

Before we were married, he had tunnel vision when it came to work. The product had his name on it, and that mattered. He was driven, and he acknowledged that. When he asked me to marry him, he was concerned about how I would feel about that. He knew how his mind worked—and worked and worked and worked.

Leo told me several times, "I'm sorry I can't play. Go to the movies with your friends. Go to church with your family." He had a new idea, and he wanted to work on it. That was his life, and I understood. I had a very full life with family, friends, and an active church life, so I was always happy that Leo was doing what he loved.

Leo discussing a guitar with a new guitar player

Leo was very neat and organized. Everything was in its place, and he knew where everything was. He made sure that every nut and bolt in his laboratory was kept organized. I tend to be a little sloppy— actually, I am very sloppy, but, thankfully he put up with me, as long as he kept his home office organized.

His desk was always neat, neat, neat. His drafting table was neat, neat, neat, and his work bench in the laboratory was always perfect.

He always had his "peepers," which is what we called the magnifying glasses that he put over his glasses. He had certain types of tools that he used for everything. His nuts and bolts were in his old tuna cans. He did not like anything to be messy.

It was a puzzle why Leo married me because he was so neat, and I am messy. My motto is, "My house is clean enough to be healthy, but messy enough to be happy!" I am lovable, so it all evens out.

Leo was always very punctual, and he was always first in line. If someone was late, he would stare at them and say something like, "You know, we need to get busy now, and you'd better be on time. We have a schedule going. We have to keep this schedule." He was the same way with his timeliness at home, especially if you were talking about food.

Leo's lab

Leo would say, "This is what I want done, and this is how it's going to be done." And, "I need it by four o'clock." And then, most of the time he just left the workers alone. He would wander out through the plant periodically just to be sure everybody was doing something, but he did not look over their shoulders constantly. He just expected everyone to do their job.

If Leo found out that an employee had been "borrowing" things and not bringing them back or stealing guitars, they were gone in a second. He could not stand laziness. He fired several people over the years, and I was surprised with a couple of them. They seemed to be nice people. But he said, "No, their work is just not my kind of work." He would not put up with slovenly workers, guys that would come drunk or too tired from a hangover from partying the night before. You simply did not do that around Leo. You came ready to work.

Leo's desk was always perfectly neat

Leo would come out of his lab and say something like, "OK, we're making number 4732. Today, I want fourteen of them. Three of this, and that color. And they had best be ready by four o'clock." He was somewhat demanding, but again he only wanted what was best.

I enjoyed going to the plant so much. I used to go down to the factory and have potlucks with the fellows and girls in the back, and often I would bring pies from Marie Callendar's or Polly's. We would eat, laugh, and carry on. It was a jolly time that I remember fondly. There were a lot of Hispanic workers that would bring in wonderful food. The ladies and I used to tease Leo that we were going to picket out in front of the company if he did not have another potluck within the next couple months. Everybody would laugh, and Leo would say, "You guys, get back to work!" We would respond, "No, we don't want to!" He would laugh.

He had a pretty friendly way with everybody, but he was firm. He did not put up with anything. If workers were messing around, he would quickly shut it down. He would walk up to them, and say, "You know, this is not right."

It would be a big mistake to confuse Leo's easy-going nature for weakness. But Leo was patient with honest mistakes. One time, someone at the plant owned up to making a very big, costly mistake. Leo walked up and asked what was going on; the man explained his mistake. Leo just said, "I wish you knew how often I make a mistake." And then he walked off.

Some of the employees would take home scrap wood for beach bonfires or make chopping blocks for the kitchen. This tickled Leo, he hated to see waste and being so frugal, he loved to see things get used up. I think the thing that upset him the most was waste, any kind of waste. He would always say, "Be careful with that, it can be used for something else, or be careful not to tear that, it is still good for something, or be careful with that, I plan to make something out of that." It all looked like trash to me, but he knew exactly what he was going to do with it. His German family was very concerned about wastefulness. He always looked for opportunities to recycle something into something else, and he liked everyone else to do the same.

THIRTY-MINUTE LUNCHES

Leo believed that thirty minutes was long enough for lunch. There were places around the plant that he liked, and, in particular, he liked Carl's Jr. and Spires. He would take two or three people from the office, usually George, Dale, sometimes me, or whoever happened to be around.

Leo's lunch time routine was the exact opposite of my father's, who ate *so* slowly that the rest of the family would be finished and just be sitting there. We all stayed at the table until he was finished.

Leo dreaming up a new guitar, this was his bliss!

But Leo had his own rules, and forget trying to change him. If you were late getting started and you were not finished with your meal in thirty minutes, then you had to get up from the table and go back to work anyway. You just had to leave your lunch on the table or stuff it into a doggie bag. Leo insisted that lunch be exactly thirty minutes, and he timed it.

One time, this fellow had ordered something that took a little longer than usual. Leo said, "Okay, guys, it's time to get back to work." So, two guys walked out with Leo and the other guy was trying to get his lunch to go. Leo went out, started the car, and just drove off without him. They guy was yelling, "Hey! Excuse me! Excuse me!"

Leo did eventually stop, and laughingly let the guy in his car, but he said, "Thirty minutes is what lunch is supposed to be." I do not think that guy ever forgot that lesson.

FENDER AVENUE

The G&L plant is located on Fender Avenue. Leo bought the vacant land, and at the time the street had no name. Leo built all of the industrial buildings on that street, except for the property that fronts State College Boulevard in Fullerton.

When Leo went into the city's offices, the Fullerton planning department said, "Well, Mr. Fender you can name the street anything you want." Leo just hemmed and hawed. He could not come up with a name for the street.

Leo was indecisive, and after taking a while to think about it, the city planners finally said, "We're just going to name it Fender Avenue." Leo said, "Oh, no!"

"Yeah," they said. "We're going to name it Fender Avenue." And it is still named that to this day.

PRE-CBS FENDER

There is a perception that pre-CBS Fender guitars are better, but that is just plain false.

The notion that pre-CBS instruments were superior to instruments during the CBS era is really an urban myth—propagated mainly by Fender competitors and dealers of vintage instruments. While there were issues at CBS, they were mainly issues involving the executive management. Truthfully, the CBS executives hit Leo like a truck on the executive level. But the actual production of the guitars was the same or perhaps even better.

Fender guitar designer Freddie Tavares worked at Fender in both pre- and post-CBS years, and he would never have tolerated any decline in quality. He had worked with Leo too long to allow that. Don Randall, who established a genius sales organization at Fender, later left the company and started a competing line of Randall-brand amplifiers. Even as a competitor in 1978, Don told in *Guitar Player* magazine, "The rumors are completely unfounded. CBS is a very proud company, and the emphasis was always on product improvement, doing a better job for the public."

Leo inventing with his peepers!

Many people do not realize that even after Leo sold to CBS, Leo remained working with them for many years. Not only was Leo there, but the company had the exact same production line, and the same craftsmen remained in place.

When the plant moved to Corona and Mexico in 1985, the head of the research and development department, Pete Bell, said, "I know the guys from the plant who had moved down to Mexico, and they were true experts. Fender did not lose any quality down in Mexico. In fact, in some ways, the instruments were better because they did not have all the hassle of California's over-regulation."

While the guitars themselves did not suffer by moving to Corona or Mexico, the decision to move out of Fullerton was not popular with Leo or the rest of the core people. Fullerton was Leo's hometown.

The bright side is that G&L, Leo's final company, maintains a distinct, historical mark in the industry, and it has remained in Fullerton through the years. The plant is virtually unchanged from the way Leo established it himself. In fact, out of respect for Leo, the current owners maintain Leo's office and lab exactly as it was the day he died. I am so honored to be their Honorary Chairman at G&L to this day. The people are wonderful, and their hand-craftsmanship is a purist's dream. G&L makes guitars that are just stunning.

I love both Fender and G&L; they are both Leo's "sons." Today, I have good relationships with the executives of both companies. Both companies make beautiful instruments, and Leo is smiling down upon both of his children!

LES PAUL

Leo once publicly said that he really liked musician Roy Clark. A reporter quickly chimed in and said, "But doesn't he usually play a Gibson?" Laughing, Leo shot right back, "Well, we all can't have the best!"

Often business owners try to create barriers for their competition or try to keep their ideas to themselves. Yet, Leo had his own style. While Fender and Gibson may have been competitors in the eyes of the world, Leo and Les Paul were actually good friends. I know that Les gave Leo some advice that really was helpful, and I am sure it was reciprocated.

Leo came out with his electric guitars years before Gibson, but Leo always thought that Gibson guitars were beautifully made and he admired them. Leo spent many Sundays with Les Paul at his home out in the Los Angeles area. He would go over; they would sit out on the porch, and drink lemonade and talk. "What do you think is gonna be the newest kind of instrument?" or "What are you doing on yours? This is what I'm doing on mine." It was a great friendship, and he went there quite regularly.

They would share ideas about how to improve their instruments, get different tones and share what worked. It did not bother Leo that Les was making electric guitars, and they were selling wonderfully. Les' guitars were different than his. For what Les Paul wanted it to do, he did it perfectly.

Les Paul's instrument was there, and Leo's was over here. They were different. I never understood the difference, because it was technical, but I was glad that Leo had the friendship. They were in the same business, but they did not have the same guitar. Leo thought that, as long as Les could sell his guitars, and Leo could sell his, everybody was happy!

Leo was very fond of Les, and vice versa. Years ago, soon after Leo died, I was listening to a nighttime radio show, and they were interviewing Les Paul on the program. They were not necessarily interviewing him about Leo, but the subject of their friendship came up. Les said that they had had a good relationship and that he did make a good guitar.

Leo would joke with Les, and say things like, "Well, there's always room for number two!" Both Leo and Les were after the same thing. They both wanted to make the music world better — to make the world better through music. I do not think Leo ever thought of Les as a competitor.

Both Leo and Les were very bright people, and they both had class. They knew that guitar players were not limited to having just one guitar. Guitar players should have lots of guitars! They each had their own place in the industry, and they were both successful. Leo thought that Gibsons were beautiful instruments, and he was very happy for Les' success.

Leo's lab

LEO AND MONEY

In business, Leo was frugal and money was not his key motivation. He told *Guitar Player* magazine,

> *I always felt that even if you had some items that were not too profitable, you should have them anyway in order to provide a full dealer selection. So at Fender, we always produced some items that were marginal, or even slightly red ink, so that dealers and customers would have a large selection of merchandise.*

If Leo were sitting here and heard that the number one piece of music memorabilia was a Fender Stratocaster that sold for $2.7 million dollars in 2005, he would take a few deep breaths. He would be slightly amazed. He would not take credit for it.

He would say, "I never thought we would sell so many." Yet he would also say, "Of course they sold." He knew how wonderful they were. If somebody wants to spend that much money, good for them, but he would not be taking personal credit.

If Leo heard that a run-of-the mill Fender Stratocaster built in 1959 routinely sells for twenty-five or thirty-five thousand dollars, he would probably laugh. I know he would have said, "Well, I wouldn't pay that much for it, I'm glad that someone did."

I think he would be amazed—kind of grateful, but not particularly surprised—at the praise his vintage guitars get, and how they sell for such high prices. He was very proud of his instruments; they were the children that he and Esther never had.

Leo's business earned a fortune; however, it has always been interesting that for building an iconic, worldwide empire, the driving force was Leo's love for musicians. Money never motivated him, and he had very little interest in it. Leo had been poor in his younger years, and later he was very comfortable, but he remained just the same, steady person through it all.

LEO ON LEADERSHIP

Leo was arguably one of history's finest leaders. While he was not the slick CEO type, Leo was certainly an iconic inventor and thought leader, as well as a spectacular business leader. His small, Fullerton-based venture grew so large that today it is a worldwide, household name.

Often, the leader of a startup company is replaced when the enterprise goes large. Not so for Leo, as he had a rare blend of skills to run his business at all stages of its growth. On top of that, Leo was proficient at every job held by his 1,000-plus employees. As the cherry on top, Leo was inducted into the Rock and Roll Hall of Fame. How many leaders can say all that? When we look at Leo's leadership style, we really hit the jackpot.

Louis Johnson and Leo Fender

Leadership breaks down into the four cornerstones of, *Me We Do Be*. *Me* is quality thinking, *We* is relationships, *Do* is productivity, and *Be* is our designs for the future. In all four areas, Leo set a high standard.

Leo's "Me" cornerstone was chronic, deep thinking.

Mark Twain said, "The two most important days in your life are the day you were born, and the day you learn why." Leo knew his *why*, and he had a laser focus on his mission, which was to put quality guitars into the hands of musicians. He believed that music made the world a better place.

Leo did not get up in the morning and then jump right into the distractions of the day. Instead, he started every morning with his long, meditative bath. Leo was intensely reflective, and cultivated long episodes of complete solitude.

Philosophically, Leo had strong ethics and core values. He was as true-blue honest as they come. He never shaded the truth, and his word was as good as gold. Leo had integrity and a sterling character, and he kept his word.

The world could be at war, the country could be in crisis, or a group of iconic rock stars could be in the next room. No matter the extremes of massive calamities or wild fame and fortune, he never got distracted. Through it all, Leo simply stayed focused and just steadily went forward.

Leo's *We* cornerstone was built on solid relationships. For someone who was naturally shy, Leo actually had a remarkably strong *We* cornerstone, and he developed strong lifelong connections.

Leo never went for big titles like "President" or "CEO." If his position ever came up, Leo would just say, "I'm the owner of the joint." He did not lead by position or title. Leo led by example.

Leo's lab

With the *We* cornerstone, many lesser leaders use their titles when introducing themselves, expecting obedience, and recruiting an inner circle of yes-men to follow their orders. Leo did the opposite. Some leaders expect a unanimous vote, but Leo thought that would be trivial. He loved critical thinking, real debate, and people who told him the way it really was.

When Leo formed G&L with George Fullerton, the "G" stood for "George," while the "L" stood for "Leo." Leo owned the company, yet he put his initial after George's. When asked about that, he would simply say, "Oh, it really doesn't matter one way or the other."

Leo usually had a slight smile on his face, and, while he was quiet, he was pleasant to be around. He never yelled or lost his temper. Leo never demanded respect. His cool, mild-mannered style naturally earned genuine respect from everyone around him.

Leo certainly had the *Do* cornerstone down cold. He was a *doer* to the point of just going nuts.

Leo was usually the first one to the plant in the morning. He did whatever was necessary to get the job done. He could do it all, and, if something broke, Leo was the first to run out and fix it. At the end of the day, Leo went home with grease under his fingernails, just like everyone else.

For Leo, dressing for success never meant suits, white shirts, and ties. Frankly, he dressed like a factory worker, and visitors to his factory often mistook him for one. He dressed to be comfortable, not to impress. While functional, his facilities were kept spic-and-span, which meant everyone could work better.

Leo sold his first company for about $300 million in today's dollars. At the time, he was living in a mobile home because he liked its simplicity. With millions in the bank, he just stayed there. Leo had no interest in impressing anyone.

The *Be* cornerstone centers on setting goals, time management, and creating a legacy.

Leo's goal for the future was clear-cut—to make the perfect guitar. When time management became the craze, Leo's time management system was simply to, "Work all the time."

Leo literally designed the future of music on his drafting table.

There he imagined a future where every guitarist around the world had the sound and look they wanted. That was his legacy.

Even for Leo, work had its limits. He enjoyed his hobbies of cameras and ocean cruising. Leo put family first, and the greatest moment in life was to hold a new grandbaby.

The core team at Fender

CHAPTER 10

Around the World
with Leo

WORKIN' AND A-CRUISIN'

Every year, Leo and I took at least one cruise somewhere around the world. It was just wonderful!

On a cruise, there were times when Leo was very relaxed. On some cruises, he was so relaxed that he did not even take his pencils and pens out very often. I thought everything was nice. He was not in any rush. Then there would be other times when he would constantly be drawing and drawing, or writing and writing, and wanting to get to the next port so he could use the telephone to call George or Dale. So, we had both kinds of cruises.

Leo really enjoyed our trip to Greece. We enjoyed sitting up on the Parthenon together and laughing over our accomplishment in making it all the way to the top! It was not an easy climb, and there was no railing on the side of the very narrow walkway.

Leo and I joked that the best way to get rid of excess tourists was to let them fall right off the edge. We joked that it was not a good place for older people because there are no restrooms up there.

We were amazed at the chaotic traffic. Everybody beeped their horns, constantly! They did not pay any attention to the stoplights. They just kept on going. But Leo was even more amazed at the history of the Parthenon, and we listened in on some of the guides. It was wonderful to see the city, and it was great knowing that we were not the oldest things up on that hill!

Our trip to Athens

It was wonderful seeing the world with Leo. When we were at sea, at times, I was a little sorry because it did not look like Leo was having much fun. I would be in the pool getting a suntan, or just being silly with my new friends.

Leo would be over in a corner with his same black pants, black jacket, and white hat that he went to work in, and was now on a cruise with the same clothes. He had his little pad and paper and would be designing and designing.

"Phyllis!" He would wave at me, "Come here. Come here, Phyllis."

I would say, "You ready to go to lunch or something?"

"No, you've been out in the sun too long. You need a piña colada."

"No, Leo, I don't drink."

He said, "Well, I don't drink either. But you need a piña colada."

"Leo, I'll have an iced tea."

"No, you need a piña colada" he insisted.

"Okay," I said. The waiter would come over and bring a piña colada.

Leo loved the girls!

Leo would hand it to me, and I would take a sip and immediately put it down. And that is the last I would see of the piña colada. He would drink the whole thing. In Leo's mind, he did not drink because he ordered the drink for his wife! Then, he went back to his corner, and he would design and design all day long.

We spent most of our time on the sun deck, where I would be out by the swimming pool getting a suntan—and probably skin cancer!

Leo would be back under the sundeck. He would be writing in the little notebook that he always carried with him—writing and writing and writing. He just could not stop working. He could not get his mind off what he was going to discover next.

Leo with the Glenn Miller Band

Once Leo said, "When we get to the next port I have to get off the ship fast and find a phone booth. I've got to call the office."

I replied, "Honey, you can just call from the ship. They've got a direct line; you can call anytime."

"No," he said. "I'm just going to call from that dock."

"Leo, you could get it done and off your mind tonight if you would just call." I reminded him.

"It costs too much." He replied.

I said, "Well, you also have got to put money in the phone down on the dock. Why don't you just do it on the ship?"

"Because it costs too much." He replied again.

We laughed that he was so careful with anything that cost money for himself, even to make a simple phone call! It was just one of those little things that were built into him from a young boy. However, if he needed something for the business, he got out his checkbook without a second thought.

Our trip to Hong Kong on a floating restaurant

GERMANY

It was well-known that Leo was a certified workaholic, and sometimes it would even surprise me! The worst display of this happened on a trip to Germany for a music show.

Leo and I went to Germany, along with Dale Hyatt and his wife, Eileen. We planned on going on to Switzerland for about a week after the show.

While I love to travel and take a cruise, I hate to fly. I hate to fly! But Germany is a long cruise, and an even a longer walk. So, I just gritted my teeth, and we flew all the way to Germany. When we arrived, the four of us went out to dinner and a show, and then we just went back to our hotel rooms that first night.

Our Amazon trip up the river

The next day, we visited the show, and everyone kept saying "Leo's here! Leo's here!" As we went to the various shows, we walked up and down the aisles. There would be thousands of guitars, and Leo said, "Well, they look like mine!" He came up with a design that, as hard as people try, they cannot beat it!

We were having a good time, However, that night, all of a sudden, Leo blurted out, "I want to go home tomorrow."

"What?!" I exclaimed.

"Yeah, I—I need to go home," he said. "I've got some work I have got to do."

"Leo," I said, "Dale and Eileen—we're all going to Switzerland."

"I've got to get back to work." he said again.

"But you know how I hate to fly," I said. "If I'd known you were going to stay one day, I never would have come."

When Leo got a bee in his bonnet, it just was what it was. Leo just matter-of-factly said, "You need to change the tickets now."

I called Dale and Eileen. They too were equally stunned! We had already made all the arrangements to tour around Germany and Switzerland. But Leo was the captain, so we called the airlines and made the necessary changes.

I will never forget that flight home. Every bench seat was taken, and it was stuffed full. As luck would have it, Leo sat next to two very slender people on either side of him. On the other hand, I had two of the biggest men I have ever seen in my life on either side of me!

For the whole trip, I sat with my arms crossed, my legs crossed, and my head scrunched down. I could not move. The two men went to sleep. Leo was just looking at me and smiling. He was so happy. Leo said, "Well, we'll be home soon." Ninety-nine point nine percent of the time with Leo was fun, but this was the *worst* trip of my life. It was awful!

CHINA SILK FACTORY

On one vacation, Leo and I flew to Japan and stayed there a couple of days. Then we boarded a cruise ship and went to China. From there we took an eight-hour bus ride to Beijing. We stayed there and walked on the Great Wall for several hours.

While we were in China, we took a tour of a silk factory. They took us back into the plant, and it was massive. There were people working everywhere on sewing machines. They had foot-powered treadles and other gadgets on top of the machines.

A trip to China where Leo wanted to fix everything

The guides told us that we had about an hour. We were walking all around, and the tour lady was telling us all about the plant. Finally, she said, "Well, we need to get back on the bus in fifteen minutes." She asked, "Where is your husband, Mrs. Fender?"

"Oh!" I said. "He was right here just a few minutes ago."

"We need to be on that bus in fifteen minutes." She insisted.

There were hundreds of people in this huge room. I looked and looked. I called out, "Leo! Leo!" Other people on the tour even started looking for him. I walked up and down aisle after aisle, looking and looking for Leo.

Finally, I came to an aisle, looked down, and saw a pair of familiar-looking shoes peeking out from under a sewing machine.

"Leo," I said, "what are you doing?" He was down underneath one of the treadle sewing machines. A man was working on the machine up top, and Leo was down there on the ground with his pencil out and a piece of paper.

The Great Wall of China

I said, "Leo, we have to leave in just a few minutes." He paid no attention. Finally, I kicked him on his foot and said, "Leo, we're going to miss the bus!"

At last, Leo climbed out and got up. "If they let me work here for a month," he said, "I could really fix this business. They would be so successful if they just let me work here one month."

The tour lady came to me finally. "Did you find him?"

"Yeah, there he is!" I announced.

She blurted, *"Get him on the bus!"*

THE CAPTAIN'S TABLE

When we were on a cruise, we always tried to find a table where there were a lot of regular people. Leo did not like a lot of pomp and ceremony. He liked ordinary people. The funny thing is that Leo considered himself to be ordinary! Sitting with regular people, we would get to know them and hear all sorts of interesting things. One time, the cruise people had seen Leo's name on the ship's manifest.

Leo at the captain's table

They said, "Congratulations, you're going to sit at the captain's table tonight!"

"Are you sure?" I asked. I knew Leo was not going to be talking to anybody. He barely talked to the people around the regular table.

They said, "Yes! The captain would be honored to have you sit at his table!"

I told Leo about the invitation to the captain's table, and he was not happy. We sat down, and the staff served us. We had eaten half a meal, and the captain started regaling us with stories of his past cruises and voyages around the world. He told of wonderful things they had seen or people they had met, and on and on. I looked over at Leo, and he had his pen out of his pocket. He was writing on a linen napkin with his pen! He had gotten an idea about a guitar.

"Leo... Leo!" I whispered. *"Stop it. Stop it. Stop it. Stop it."*

He just kept drawing on it.

"Listen to what the captain's saying!," I begged. He listened for a little while. But when I looked over again, he was again drawing on the napkin. "Leo, that ink is never gonna come out of the napkin!"

Near the North Pole!

Suddenly, Leo just stood up and left. He did not say "goodnight." He did not say "goodbye." He did not say "thank you." He just left. There I was, just sitting with the captain and the other people around the table. I did not see him again for three hours. When I got back to the cabin, Leo was just in there on the table, designing another guitar.

CHAPTER 11

Retirement? Are You Kidding?

LEO TOUGHS IT OUT

Leo always loved to work and work. For him, none of it was really work, since he enjoyed it so much. I never even considered asking him about retirement. If I had, I suppose he would just look at me with a baffled, blank look on his face, and ask, "Are you kidding?" Even though old age had brought on a new set of challenges, Leo just kept going. The notion of slowing down was simply out of the question.

Leo had a slight heart condition. He saw a doctor periodically and took some medications. It did not slow him down at all. After being married for about three or four years, I noticed that he was stumbling. Usually, when he walked, he walked with purpose. But, I noticed that Leo had begun walking a little differently.

I mentioned this to his heart doctor, and he decided that Leo needed to see a neurologist in Fullerton. They did some testing, and they monitored him for a while. The stumbling thing got a little worse. Finally, the doctors determined that Leo had Parkinson's disease. He saw the neurologist periodically, and, was prescribed more medicines. With Parkinson's there is not a lot you can do, except to live with it the best you can, and for as long as you can. He also developed Bulbar Palsy, which meant he could not swallow on his own. That was really a disappointment for a man like Leo, who loved to eat.

Leo had a few accidents where he fell, one time in the bathtub. He hit the back of his head on the tile wall. Luckily, our two sons were visiting that day, and they lifted him out of the tub, and there was blood on the wall. We got him to the doctor. He said, "You've got to be more careful with him." As long as he was seated, he was fine. It never affected his brain or his thinking power. It affected his writing. It got tiny, tiny, tiny.

Later his speech got a little impaired, but it progressively got worse. By the end of his life, he sort of mumbled, and there were times near the end when the guys at the plant would call me and say, "Leo's trying to tell us something. It seems important to him, and we can't understand him." I would drive down to the plant, and I'd say, "Talk to me, Honey. What is it?" I had listened carefully to his speech at home, so I could still understand him. I would repeat what he told me, and he would nod as if to indicate, "That's what I'm trying to say."

It was sad to experience. Leo was frustrated, but he was not angry. He was frustrated because there was so much more he wanted to do. He could tell he was losing his ability to get things done. His mind was fine, but he was losing the ability to get his ideas down on paper or tell somebody what to do. That was frustrating for him because he had been in charge of everything for many decades.

Everything Leo did, owned, or designed was born from his ideas, and he was losing the ability to communicate those ideas. That was very hard for him. He was always quiet, but now he had no choice. It was a deafening quiet.

In his final days, Leo's Parkinson's Disease got worse. The men from the plant would come up every day, and I would get him ready. At that time, I fed him through a tube in his stomach. I dressed him, bathed him, and all that. And they would come up, take him down to the plant for two or three hours, and then they would bring him back to the house. I would take those clothes off, put his black sweats on, and then he would sit in his chair and still try to work. Leo's handwriting got so miniature that you could hardly see it. I was the only one that could decipher it.

Leo and his Country Music Association's Pioneer Award

As Leo's Parkinson's progressed, he required a lot of care. I used to tease him about it and say, "See, it was a good thing you married a young wife, 'cause now I can do all these things for you, and it's free!" He would smile. If he had married someone more of his own age, she would not have been able to care for him. I fed him through the tube in his stomach three times a day, gave him a sponge bath, dressed him, and make sure his pills got down his food tube.

Our last public event together was a Buck Owens concert at the Crazy Horse Saloon, a theater in Orange County. George and Lucille Fullerton were with us. Leo really loved Buck, so he had a beautiful red, white, and blue guitar made to give to him. Buck was just thrilled, both with having Leo there and with the guitar. Buck got a table for all of us right up front, took the guitar up on stage, tuned it up, and played it that night. It sounded beautiful, and Buck talked about Leo throughout the show.

Leo with Buck Owens at his final public appearance, February 27, 1991

After the show, Leo and Buck sat together and visited. Leo was frail but so happy, and Buck was just beaming from ear to ear. Leo really enjoyed his music. The night was perfect. Leo loved musicians and created electric guitars so that they could be heard. It was fitting that his last night out was spent joyfully listening to the wonderful music created by one of his instruments.

Buck Owens playing his new G&L guitar

Soon after that, I had gotten Leo fed and ready for bed. Leo was not one who said "thank you" very often. It was not that he was mean, I already knew he was thankful. One night, in particular, he took my hand, put it up to his face, and said, "I finished what I was supposed to do." A few days later, he said, "I know this has been hard for you." He said, "Thank you. Thank you for helping me."

It was fulfilling because I knew that Leo had completed his life's mission. How many of us can say that? It was a very touching and special moment to have with him.

Most of us *know* what we should be doing. A few of us get to accomplish it, a lot of us do not. Sometimes we get a little bit of both. Leo knew what he was supposed to do, and he completed his life's work. He had a wife who loved him and who was able to help him. It was good.

LEO'S LAST GUITAR

Leo's passion was to build the perfect guitar. In his mind, he did not have any competition. His "babies" were being so well received. Leo did not think of his instruments as being art, as many people do, but he thought of them as being perfect. His joy came from perfection.

Leo was pleased that something that was such a delight to create was so well-accepted at dances and concerts. He was pleased to know that they were being enjoyed, that they brought so much happiness. He did not talk much about his guitars at home, other than when a song came on the TV or radio, being played on a Fender or G&L guitar, and he would just say, "It's really sounding good. It's really sounding good."

It seemed like so many of the musicians were using his instruments. You would see them on TV and in movies. You looked at the band on screen, and you would see all Fender equipment. That gave him the knowledge that he was doing it right. The other guy may have a different idea or a different plan for his instruments. Leo *knew* what he wanted to do with his instruments. He did not worry about the other guy. If the other guy made a good guitar, then that was good for the music industry. He felt if they were smart, they would be playing one of his!

All the designs were his inventions. Leo never bought a competitor's guitar and tried to copy them. Fender guitars came first, and many copied his work. Other designers would see how the instrument looked and sounded, and that was fine for them. But for Leo, he wanted his instruments to be distinctively his. He was proud of them.

By his own estimate, Leo accumulated between fifty and seventy patents. In the Fullerton Museum, there is a display showing the *last* guitar that Leo ever made. That was special. It has never been put into production. He looked it over and blessed it the night before he died.

The guys had brought it in from the plant and he held it in his lab. They said they would take it out in the plant and polish it, and then leave it on his table to look at in the morning.

Like Leo, this instrument is very unusual. The current G&L owners do not know exactly what to do with it, because it is so different. It is not a standard guitar, but it is not a bass either. It is kind of a cross between a guitar and a bass, and the problem is that they really do not know what it is. The G&L executives just say, "We don't know how to sell it." It would have been nice if he had lived a little longer, so he could tell us about it." But then again it would be nice if he had lived a little longer, period.

I would have liked to have known his reasoning because he did not seem to have explained it to anybody. He seemed to be proud of it. He declared it completed the night before he died. It is Leo's last mystery.

WHY? SERIOUSLY, WHY?!

His entire life, Leo always worked an insane schedule.

It started early. In the 1940s, Doc Kauffman, one of Leo's earliest business partners, left Leo's company because Leo worked from seven in the morning to two the next morning. Leo operated on just three or four hours of sleep. Leo was like a human convenience store; he was always open. On the other hand, Doc wanted to have a normal life and spend time with his wife and kids. They always remained friends, but frankly, they separated their business interests primarily over Leo's crazy schedule. Leo was simply obsessed, and most of the people around him wanted a bit more balance in their lives.

One day we were both at home, and Leo was fixated on designing a new guitar. With a heart full of love for this man, I quietly looked at him, and in a calm voice, I asked him, "Leo, why are you so driven? Why are you such a workaholic?" He just sat there; I asked again, "Leo… Why… Really Leo… Why?" Leo hesitated, he had a bashful look on his face. I asked again, "Leo, why?"

Finally, after a long silence, Leo whispered, "I had a dream many years ago."

"Well, I like dreams," I said. What happened in your dream?"

He replied, "Jesus talked to me."

"Jesus talked to you? That's wonderful! What did Jesus say?"

Leo said, "Jesus told me to do this."

I was so surprised. Leo never talked like that. Leo never mentioned anything religious at all. But I am a Christian, so I said, "Okay, Leo please tell me about it."

Then Leo told me something I will never forget. He said, "In my dream, Jesus told me that this world was going to be a very tough place. He told me that he had sent angels to the earth. He called these angels "musicians," and they make the world more bearable and bring joy. Jesus told me that my gift was not to be a musician. He had different plans for me. He also said there was a reason I was not a musician. He told me that my purpose in life was to design and build guitars for those angels."

Leo got his orders that night. I simply said, "Okay, Leo. Now I understand." Now it all made sense. The world needs music to make it better, and that is what drove him. I always supported him in that vision.

For the rest of Leo's life, he kept working and working. Occasionally, he would quietly kiss my hand and remind me, "You know why I am doing this."

LEO AND JESUS

It was interesting, even though Leo had told me about his dream, it never lead to any discussion about church or religion in general. It just helped me understand the man's pure motivation behind his obsession with inventing. Now, I simply understood.

Leo and me on our Anniversary

Leo had abandoned Christianity early in life, and he was non-religious for most of his life. On the other hand, I am a Christian, and I attend church regularly. I have a "live and let live" attitude. With Leo or anyone else for that matter, I never push my beliefs; however, I certainly have never been bashful about being a Christian either. Leo knew that I had Jesus. I love the Lord, and I love all the wonderful Biblical teachings!

Occasionally, I would ask Leo to come to church with me when I was singing in the choir, or doing something that I wanted to share with him. Everyone from church knew Leo from his faithful attendance at all the church potluck dinners, but there were never any religious discussions.

One day Leo and I were home, and Leo came out of his office area in his wheelchair just weeping, and tears just streaming down his face. I immediately became alarmed, because I thought that he was sick, in pain, or something. I rushed up to him, dropped to my knees, and looked at his face. I cried, "Leo, what's wrong?! Leo, what's wrong?!" Leo just kept crying, and I was in shock wondering what to do. I said, "Do I need to call for help? Are you sick?"

Finally, Leo was able to hold back his weeping long enough to say, "Tell me about *your* Jesus!" he asked several times. Now I was really in shock! Leo never talked this way. This was just not like Leo.

I said, "Ok, sure, I will tell you about my Jesus." And I did. I told Leo how I loved the Lord. I told him that I loved how Jesus had created the whole earth, but he lived so simply and humbly. I talked about how Jesus loves all the little children, and how he just wants us all to be kind to each other. I told him how Jesus had suffered for all our sins and all the stupid things we do, so if we accept him, he can remove all that garbage from our lives. Jesus is all things good, and I love and adore Him.

Leo listened intently. Then he asked, "How do I get all of this for myself?"

"Just accept him," I responded.

True to Leo, he then asked, "How much does it cost?"

"Leo, it does not cost anything. It is already paid for by Jesus. It's a gift; you just have to accept that gift."

Leo said, "I believe in Jesus. What do I do?"

I told Leo, "Let's pray together." And then I walked Leo through a salvation acceptance prayer, and Leo prayed along, repeating after me. This was the most tender, sweet moment I ever had with Leo. I love Leo, and I love the Lord, and now Leo did too.

Leo had always lived like a Christian, and now he was an authentic Christian. Leo was quiet, kind, honest, and he was never hypocritical or judgmental. I saw Leo interact with hundreds of people year after year from every kind of diverse background, age, race, religion, sexual orientation, and financial level. Think about it; you will never find a more diverse, eclectic group on planet Earth than you find in the music industry! Never once did Leo mutter a single negative word about anyone. Leo was purely "live and let live," and he enjoyed helping every single one of them.

In his Leo kind of way, his guitars were his expression of love to everyone around him. He just wanted everyone to make the music they enjoyed, and he was content being in the background and helping to make it all possible. From that day on, instead of only having a love for music and our family, Leo also started talking about his love for Jesus.

LEO LEAVES THE WORLD HE CHANGED

On March 20, 1991, at the age of 81, Leo got up, and despite his long suffering from Parkinson's Disease, he did what Leo always did. He got up to go to work. Leo thought that the idea of retirement was a joke. That was for wimps. Leo may have needed to use a wheelchair by then, but he was no wimp.

Before going to the office that day, I helped him get dressed. Of course, the thinking was already done on that topic. He would go to the office as usual, and it did not matter how poorly he felt. Leo went with his usual black shoes and socks, black pants and belt, a white shirt, and his black windbreaker. I drove Leo down to Fender Avenue to the door of his humble office and lab at G&L.

Leo spent all day in his favorite place, his lab, a small room with no windows, sprayed popcorn ceilings and florescent lights, working at his two military-green workbenches. Here he had spent years getting his instruments tweaked to give the musicians just the feel they wanted. Some of his colleagues noticed that Leo was not doing too well, but he brushed off all their suggestions to go home. He was white-knuckle determined to finish his day's work. Finally, the men called me to tell me they were bringing him home and told me that Leo was struggling and really needed some rest. They brought him home, and helped get him into bed because he was so weak. Later I checked on him, gave him a sponge bath, and his food and medications through his feeding tube. He wanted to go to bed earlier than usual that night. I knew he did not feel well, and I checked on him every hour until I fell asleep.

Leo died in our home in Fullerton. I knew something was wrong as soon as I woke up because it was so quiet, Leo could not speak by this time, but he still made noises, either as he slept or when he was awake. That is when I noticed he was on the floor. Apparently, he had gotten up to get ready for work. I called 911, even though I knew he was already gone.

They asked me, "Do you know CPR?"

"Yes," I said. I knew Leo might someday need it, and I wanted to be able to help, so I took a course for it.

They said, "Then I want you to start CPR."

"No, he's already gone," I said. "He's not here anymore."

"We still want you to do it." They insisted.

I did not know it at the time, but Leo's doctor happened to be at the 911 call center when the call came in. When he heard it was for Leo Fender, he knew without a doubt it was Leo's heart.

I did CPR for about fifteen to twenty minutes. It felt like forever, until they got to our house. They came in and immediately forced me to leave the room, even though I wanted to stay with Leo. They later came out to the living room where some family members had gathered by then, and they asked me a bunch of questions.

"Was he feeling ill?" they asked. He had fallen on the floor in front of the heater, so it was hard for them to tell when he might have died because he was still warm. The police came, and the fire engines came. The street was blocked off. The neighbors all ran out to see what was happening. The coroner finally came after many hours, took him, and I never saw him again.

He had fallen, but the doctors said that he had died before he hit the floor. He had had a massive heart attack. God kindly took him home quickly, and he did not suffer for a second.

Our family laid Leo to rest at Fairhaven Memorial Park in Santa Ana, California. The first Mrs. Fender, Esther, and her brother and a couple of other family members, and Leo had bought plots at Fairhaven in Santa Ana. I wanted him to be there with Esther. People said, "Well, you're Mrs. Fender now." I said, "It doesn't matter, he was married to Esther for forty-five years." She is buried there with him. That was good. I was glad that we could do that for them.

We had the funeral at Fairhaven, where Esther also had her funeral. I thought that was appropriate. We had good friends, good music, and a small funeral. It was raining that day. We still walked down behind the casket to his burial. We had a short graveside service since it was raining. We went back to our house, and the family stayed around. There were a lot of reporters and people standing outside, and watching what was going on around the house.

Then we, as a family, tried to move forward. We had two services for Leo. One was at the University of California at Irvine. It was an unusual grouping. Because of his Parkinson's Disease, he had become involved with an organization that worked for a cure and gave out information on new medicines. It was a charity memorial, and many people attended. I spoke, as did many others.

We had a smaller, family service at Temple Baptist Church in Fullerton, for his closest friends and family. This was for those who knew and loved Leo, including many musicians and people who had worked with him. There was a lot of music. Many people wanted to dedicate songs to him. It was very difficult for me to speak that day. Most of those that spoke were longtime friends and musicians. It was very emotional, and I was very pleased that they cared so much for him because these were people that he had known for a long time, mostly in the music industry.

At his funeral, I made sure they placed his plastic pocket holder with all his miniature tools in his shirt pocket under his jacket. Somehow it just did not seem right for him to be all dressed up and not have his tools with him. That was Leo.

Leo and me heading out for an Anniversary dinner

You never know! Maybe Leo would run into an angel that needed his harp tuned up, and Leo would continue his work in heaven!

When Leo died, Fender historian Tom Wheeler wrote,

> *The moment I heard of Leo Fender's death, I happened to be holding a Telecaster. I mention this not because it's so oh-wow*

cosmic, but for the opposite reason. Actually, the odds that anyone reading this might be holding a Fender at any given moment are probably pretty good. And yet it really wasn't so long ago when the very idea of solid-body instruments seemed undignified, even preposterous. "Plank" guitars, they called them. Leo Fender ... changed all that.

Nobody outside of Southern California music circles heard much about Leo Fender until he'd been making guitars for nearly two decades. They'd heard of his guitars all right, but Leo was too wrapped up in his work to pursue or even to consider the spotlight for himself.

Leo's accomplishments for "contributions of outstanding technical significance to the recording field" were acknowledged with a Grammy Award in 2009, the year he would have been one-hundred years old. Leo did not do it for the awards, he did not do it for money, and he certainly did not do it for fame. Leo Fender did it all for the angel musician that had a gift and needed to be heard.

CHAPTER 12

Just Be Yourself and Enjoy the Music

On many levels, the story of Leo Fender is profound. When Leo invented the electric guitar, people laughed at him. Ultimately their sales put Fender number one in the world. Later he told me, "Maybe they've changed their minds!"

My Leo's journey includes a spectrum ranging from silly stories to iconic inventions, to a touching message of spiritual strength. Throughout it all, my Leo was just being himself, and looking back on his life it seems so logical the way it all came together. Despite having a glass eye, being deaf and somewhat shy, he was always content just being himself. It is a story that motivates and inspires each of us as we seek our own life's journey.

Leo was indeed intensely driven by his calling to the point of being a severe workaholic. In the 1970s, Freddie Tavares was quoted to say, "He'd been working too hard all his life anyway. He didn't know how to relax, how to play. All he knew was work." Freddie was right, at least until kids and grandkids came into his life.

Over time, Leo changed his workaholic ways, and his simple farm boy roots and simple tastes came through once again. Through it all, his world was full of odd quirks involving blenders, cans of tuna, carrot juice, and white cars. Like many historic figures, my Leo had an abundance of goofy habits, alongside a simple confidence to be himself.

Keith Richards and Phyllis Fender when Leo was inducted into the Rock and Roll Hall of Fame

My Leo was quiet, but he was not weak. He was confident and never second-guessed himself. He would not put anything on the market until he felt it was perfect. Once one of his guitars would go on the market, he would immediately set out to make the next one even more perfect.

In all my years with Leo, and since then, I have never met a person or heard about anyone that did not like Leo. How many people can say that? Whatever anyone thinks they know about my Leo, the reality was that he built an iconic empire, where his work has literally touched every person on the planet. He did it by calmly being himself.

Later in life, the only thing that really, fully captured Leo's attention, even more than guitars and girls in tight jeans, were the grandchildren. He would just stare at them and smile. He was always happy to see the kids running around the house, making noise at Christmas, and family get-togethers. He loved to see them jump in the pool and swim; he would sit there just watch them with a big smile on his face. Leo was a wonderful grandfather. He would just cry when the grandchildren had to leave our house to go home. He would ask, "Why can't they stay longer? Why can't they?" I would reply, "Well Leo, we've got to allow them to go to bed once in a while."

I was able to see a Leo with all his brilliance and all his fame and fortune. And then I saw the Leo who was so tender that, when he held our grandbabies, he would have tears in his eyes.

Leo and Phyllis Fender on their last Anniversary together

The secret to understanding Leo was that he never did a single thing in his life to impress others. He preferred his everyday work clothes over suits or tuxes. He liked sitting at the table of regular folks on a cruise, rather than sitting at the captain's table. Even with lots of money in the bank, he was happy living in a modest mobile home. All I had to do to get Leo excited was to tell him the grandkids were coming over or that we were eating out at Sizzler for dinner. For all his brilliance in his lab, he liked his home life simple. I do not know a better word to describe our life together.

When you saw the inside of our day-to-day life, you might notice that my Leo subtly created an environment that allowed a connection between an older generation of mechanical engineers with pocket protectors and a younger generation of stars and aspiring stars. Fender and G&L created a means by which people of different ages and backgrounds respected and supported each other. It was quite beautiful to witness, and to Leo, it was just the way things should be. I am always amazed at the variety of people that are Leo fans. I do not think Leo ever fully appreciated how rare it is to touch such a wide variety of people.

Inside those plants, it was common to see the world's greatest musicians sitting for hours with mechanical engineers talking about the tweaks to get just the vibe they wanted. There were no lights, no pictures, no autographs, and no VIP rooms. Just concrete floors, military-green work benches and a pure, common agenda to get the right sound. Leo loved creating this connection, and he did it so effortlessly.

Leo was proud of the people he worked with. He did check on them quite regularly. And he was unhappy when he saw them leaning up against the wall just talking. While Leo absolutely demanded perfection out of his employees, they loved him, and he was particularly easy to rally around and support. This was because no job was beneath him. Leo was proficient at every single job on the production line and in the plant. It was common to see Leo Fender, the great inventor and the head of a huge business, lying on a concrete floor with a wrench, fixing one of the machines.

Leo never lived large or carried any kind of air that he was the big boss. In a moment, he could be making executive calls, then just as quickly he would grab a screwdriver and go tinker on a machine. Though I admit that Leo did not hand out a lot of accolades, he did not need to. If you had a job working for Leo Fender, you knew you were good, because he demanded perfection from himself and everyone around him. You did not need to be told; you did not need a star on your forehead, a certificate of achievement, or an "employee of the month" parking space. You just knew.

My sweet Leo

The motivation behind Leo was an authentic desire to serve others. Leo was obviously a genius inventor and could have designed anything he wanted. He always carried the spark that was ignited when he noticed the poor guitarists at the war bond dance, who went unnoticed. He truly loved guitar players. He wanted to do more and more for them, literally until the day he died. Because of what Leo observed at the war bond dance in the 1940s, guitarists around the world are now being heard.

If Leo invited you to lunch, you would most likely go to Carl's Jr. for burgers and shakes. He believed that everyone would be better off with a plastic pocket protector stuffed with pencils, pens, a notepad, screwdriver, and metal ruler.

Walking through a parking lot, Leo might suddenly drop to the ground and climb under a car to check out its mechanics. He loved to see how things were designed and how they worked. One employee said, "Leo is easy to get along with because he doesn't have to impress anyone. He is a living example of what a successful man should be."

Leo's legacy has the power to baffle, inspire, and motivate. Truly, Leo's life shows us how a shy deaf guy, with a glass eye, can change the world. Leo simply never complained, and he handled his disabilities with such dignity that others around him did not even notice.

When you go to Las Vegas and visit the Hard Rock Hotel, there is a giant neon Stratocaster guitar over the entrance. Leo Fender is a world-wide, household name. However, Leo never did anything for wealth, fame or eternal neon glory. His driving motivation was far more authentic. At the deepest level, Leo was profoundly spiritual. He was motivated by something far more powerful than money or glory. As a boy, Leo had rejected Christianity when he learned that the church treasurer had taken off with the church congregation's money. Throughout his life, he made subtle hints to me and his close colleagues that he felt that God was behind the work.

It was not until his last years on earth that Leo really opened up and told me about his deeply personal dream where Jesus had told him that the world was a tough place and that musicians were really angels who were sent to make the world a little better. Shortly after Leo quietly shared this with me, he reconciled his Christian faith, and lived the rest of his life as a Christian.

Leo never bragged, he was always humble. He liked the conversation centered on the instruments, never on him. If the conversation turned to him, he would retreat. He was a workaholic until his very last day. He died getting ready to go to work.

Leo supporting the local YMCA

Leo lived a good life. He was a kind husband, father, and grandfather. He worked hard; he was honest, he did not smoke, use bad language, or lose his temper. Aside from an occasional "accidental" piña colada on a cruise, he did not drink. Leo loved to laugh big belly laughs, and we did a lot of that. He loved music, he loved musicians, and he was driven to just get instruments into their hands so that they could play. Under Leo's watch, he never wanted a musician to die with their music still inside them.

Today, the world is full of angels—also known as musicians—who make our lives better with their beautiful music. We also have the example of a truly, beautiful life.

If Leo were sitting right next to you right now, he would quietly say, "Just be yourself. Work through your challenges with dignity. The joy is not in money or fame; it is finding your passion and then just going all in and doing it. Defend your right to have your own strange quirks, just be yourself, and be sure to enjoy the music along the way."

And now, my Leo's story is finally told.

Leo Fender—
Historical Driving Tour

Leo's Birthplace and Boyhood Home
La Palma Park

1151 N. La Palma Parkway, Anaheim, California 92801
(Northeast corner of W. La Palma Avenue and N. Harbor Boulevard)

Leo was born on August 10, 1909, in a barn that once sat on this site. This is the site of the "Fender Farm," which was also known as the "Lone Oak Farm." It was located in an unincorporated area of Fullerton at the time of Leo's birth. The site was later turned into a public park and Glover Stadium, and incorporated into the City of Anaheim.

The site of the old Fender Farm where Leo was born in a barn

Leo's Elementary School
Orangethorpe Elementary School
1400 S. Brookhurst Road, Fullerton, California 92833

From start to finish, Leo only attended schools in Fullerton. His first was this elementary school that is still in use today. It was built in 1890.

Leo's Jr. High School
Wilshire Jr. High

315 E. Wilshire Avenue, Fullerton, California 92831

This school is still in use today.

Leo's High School—Fullerton High School
201 E. Chapman Avenue, Fullerton, California 92832

This school is still in use today. Leo was inducted into the school's "Hall of Fame."

Leo's College—Fullerton College (Formally Fullerton Jr. College)
3321 E. Chapman Avenue, Fullerton, California 92832

Leo attended this community college from 1923 to 1930 and graduated with an Associates Arts Degree in Accounting. Leo sat on the lawn and watched the construction of Plumber Auditorium, and the workers invited him to watch the construction work up close.

Fender Radio Shop
107 S. Harbor Boulevard, Fullerton, California 92832

Leo's first shop. This is where the world's first solid body guitar was invented. Note the historical markers on the building and the Fender guitar mural on the back wall (in the alley).

Frances Bell (Randy's Mom) and me

Me and lots of family and friends where Leo invented
today's electric guitar

Frances Bell and me in the front of Leo's first shop

Me and the National Historical Site marker at Leo's first shop

Fender Telecaster Plant
122 S. Pomona Avenue, Fullerton, California 92832

This was the site of the first mass-manufacturing plant where the Telecaster (originally called the Broadcaster) was produced. This was the world's first solid body guitar. Today the site is used as a parking garage. Note the Leo Fender murals over the entrances.

A plaque marks Leo's Telecaster plant's site

There are beautiful murals of Leo where the Telecaster plant once stood

Fullerton's school children helped design

Fender Stratocaster Plant
500 S. Raymond, Fullerton, California 92831

This building is the epicenter of the Fender revolution. This non-descript industrial plant where the Stratocaster was invented in 1953 and produced in 1954. Leo had the building designed in modules, so that if the guitar business did not work out, he had the option to lease the buildings to multiple tenants.

About every imaginable star guitar player visited this plant. Leo did not get or give autographs - it was all business. Leo opened the doors to this plant in 1953, and Pete Bell was the last one out in 1985. Pete walked through the entire plant, turned off all the lights, locked the doors and put the keys into the mail shot.

The Stratocaster was invented in 1953 in his building,
and manufactured here until 1985

Carl's Junior

1200 N. Harbor Boulevard, Fullerton, California 92830

If Leo invited you to lunch, this was probably where he would take you! Leo ate lunch here regularly. He loved the milk shakes. Note that it is located near Leo's birthplace, and just blocks from his first shop. It is also the very first Carl's Jr. ever built by Carl Karsher himself.

Right across from the Fender Farm, was Leo's favorite restaurant

A marker for the world's first Carl's Jr.

Sizzler

1401 N. Harbor Boulevard, Fullerton, California 92835

All it took to get Leo super excited, was to tell him we were going here for dinner! On special occasions, Leo enjoyed steak dinners here.

On special occasions, Leo loved to go here for dinner at Sizzler

Polly's Pie

136 N. Raymond Avenue, Fullerton, California 92831

Leo enjoyed many lunches and dinners here. He liked it because it served the "farm food" he grew up with.

Leo loved the farm food served at Polly's

G&L Plant
2548 Fender Avenue, Fullerton, California 92835

After selling Fender, Leo eventually went back to work and started G&L. He worked here until the day he passed away on March 21, 1991, at the age of 82. Today, G&L still produces electric guitars with the advanced technology that Leo designed in this building.

The G&L plant where Leo worked until the day he left the earth

Leo's Home—Cedarhill

2851 Rolling Hills Drive, Fullerton, California 92835

Even after selling Fender for $13 million in 1965 (about $300 million in today's dollar), Leo continued to live in this mobile home community. He felt it was efficient.

Leo lived in this mobile home park, he loved the simplicity

St. Jude Hospital

101 E. Valencia Mesa Drive, Fullerton, California 92835

Leo supported is hospital with grants. A portion of the cardiology section is named after him.

Leo generously supported St. Jude Hospital

YMCA

2000 Youth Way, Fullerton, California 92831

Leo loved the work of the YMCA and how it helped the youth. He supported this YMCA with grants.

Leo loved the YMCA and gave generously

Temple Baptist Church
1601 W. Malvern Avenue, Fullerton, California 92833

Leo was not religious for most of his life, but joined this church in his 70's. He loved the potluck dinners served here!

Leo's and my church

Fullerton Museum

301 N. Pomona Avenue, Fullerton, California 92832

In 1985, this museum opened a permanent display honoring Leo Fender and the Fender Guitar legacy. It has the world's first solid-body electric guitar, and the last guitar Leo handled (and many others) on display.

Fullerton Museum has a permanent Leo Fender exhibit

Signs for Fender and G&L are all around Fullerton

Leo's office and workbench on display at the Fulllerton Museum.
The Stratocaster was invented on this workbench.

Rickenbacker Plant

3895 S. Main Street, Santa Ana, California 92707

Orange County was the home of modern music. During the early 1970's, Leo worked here.

Leo worked at Rickenbacker

Fairhaven Memorial Park

1702 Fairhaven Avenu, Santa Ana, California 92705

Leo was laid to rest here by his loving family and friends. Plot: Lawn Section J. (GPS Coordinates: 33.7719002 - 117.8400269)

Family and friends gather at Leo's final resting place

We love you Leo!